Requiem for a Dream

A Repertoire of Poetic Thoughts

Dr. Boban Ramesan

Copyright © 2025 by **Dr. Boban Ramesan**

All rights reserved. No portion of this book may be reproduced in any form without written permission from the publisher or author, except as permitted by Australian Copyright Council (ACC).

This publication is designed to provide accurate and authoritative information in regard to the subject matter covered. It is sold with the understanding that neither the author nor the publisher is engaged in rendering legal, investment, accounting or other professional services. Neither the publisher nor the author shall be liable for any loss of profit or any other commercial damages, including but not limited to special, incidental, consequential, personal, or other damages.

ISBN: 978-1-923679-08-5

DEDICATION

"To, every wonder of the world,
living and dead ..."

Like a shipwrecked sailor tost
By rough waves on a perilous coast,
Lies the babe, in helplessness
And in tenderest nakedness,
Flung by labouring nature forth
Upon the mercies of the earth.

~ William Wordsworth

CONTENTS

DEDICATION ii
CONTENTS i
REQUIEM FOR A POEM 2
WIPING THE PAINT OFF THE BRUSH 4
AT THE CUSP OF A DAWN 7
THE SLEEPING FLY 12
A MAN WITH A MIND 15
THE DILUTION 18
THE MUSIC IN THE VALLEY 21
GHOSTS OF INNOCENCE 24
THE CANOPY 26
THE TRIAL 28
THE BURGLAR 30
KAFKA'S MOMENT 34
THE MAN-CHILD ON THE SHORE 36
BETRAYAL 40
THE DOOR IN THE WOODS 42
AN ABSENT PICTURE 44
THE WINTER OF YOUTH 46
A FISH-FLY 50
ICY 52
THE LAND 56
HOLE IN THE SKULL 58
RABID 61
THE MEMORIES OF A DREAM 64

TIME TRAP	67
AHEAD IN BELIEF	70
MONOCHROME	73
THROUGH THE HALF-OPEN DOOR	76
GHOST IN THE BOX	78
A MATTER OF DISTINCTION	80
UNDER THE CRIMSON SKIES	82
THE JUXTAPOSED MIRRORS	85
THE UNDERGROUND MAN	87
WHAT THE RAVEN DOESN'T KNOW	90
ANTIDOTE	93
EPILOGUE OF A EULOGY	95
ODE TO THE SCARS	98
AUTUMN MORNING	103
AT THE CORE	106
ONE AMONG OTHERS	108
WITHIN A POEM	111
FAREWELL TO A WALLABY	113
WORDLESS	115
THE UNREAD	117
THE GHOST	119
THE ENDLESS DREAM	121
A FUTURE TOO BRIGHT	123
SOCIALISATION	127
THE INJURED	128
STORIES UNTOLD	131
FURY	133
THE SACRED LIE	135

BEYOND AN AUTOGRAPH	137
TEAR DROP ON A MAPLE LEAF	139
LASTING PEACE	143
THE GHOST AND THE LAMP	146
ENCLOSED	148
TOO GOOD TO BE REAL!	151
A PLENTIFUL DAY!	153
GRIEF	156
LI"F"E	159
THE ANNIVERSARY OF A DREAM	161
THE ANNIVERSARY OF THE SOUL	165
JOURNEYING AT NIGHT	168
THE SHADOW ON THE GLASS	170
A RAIN IN THE DESERT	175
BEFORE THE END…	215
A LULLABY	220
I…	223
A NAMELESS COLOUR	224
A LETTER FROM THE QUICKSANDS	226
A POUND OF THOUGHT?	230
A DATE WITH A POT OF TEA	233
A CONFESSION	237
IF ONLY	240
NO ROOM	242
A STAR ALIVE ON EARTH	244
THE HALO OF A NIGHT	246
BETWEEN A MYTH AND A STORY	249
PHANTOM OF A GRAFFITI	253

LINES! LINES!...	258
AN ESSENTIAL JOURNEY	260
THE SHINE	263
THE CUBE	265
SAILING OVER THE LOST WORLD	268
THE BOY WHO DIDN'T SELL DREAMS	270
WRITTEN ON THE SEAS	273
A BABY DOLL	277
IT GETS DARK EARLY	278
THE RAIN AFTER THE FALL	281
A PREHISTORIC DREAM	283
THE STATE OF BEING HAPPY?	286
THE ARTFUL WAR	292
THE STORY OF THE CLOUDS	294
ON A PLATFORM ONE WINTRY NIGHT	296
WHAT THE MIRROR SAID...	299
ABOUT THE AUTHOR..	287

REQUIEM FOR A POEM

A poem hard to understand

for, it is not just made of words

but pain, that resembles pearls

born from the torment of life…

Like the conversion of a canvas

from blankness to imageries

the words spring from the wells

of translated visions of nature,

filtered through the perspective

of the writer, painting his thoughts

as an unreadable calligraphy…

The poem doesn't sell high hopes

but has melancholy written all over it,

no wonder it is so difficult to bear

like a coffin inscribed with verses,

the reader thinks he is a pallbearer

naturally he hates the thought of death

and dreads the ghosts in the graveyard

of memories hiding the untold stories…

The poem is a bitter pill to swallow

that offers no cure for the mortal pain,

Instead it makes the man more aware

of the illusion of the handsomeness

of what he perceives as the reality…

It is no panacea for his anxieties

the words are scalding for his vanity

and self-critical towards entire humanity;

he feels broken, a wistful longing

grips his heart that he can't get rid of,

till he convinces himself that he hates

the poem and would never read it again!

Out it flies through the open window

like an injured dove in the wintry darkness,

the words bleed profusely on the pavement

unheeded by the passer-by heading home;

The man is finally at peace at heart

Good riddance! he cries ecstatically

as the abandoned soul of another poem

escapes from the earth into the abyss…

WIPING THE PAINT OFF THE BRUSH

I dived into the burning orange

like a mad dove on fire

transforming into a new life

surrounded by golden flames,

amongst the orphaned waterlilies

that've sleeping in a pond of lava

since the age of timelessness…

I knew not what I've become

unfeeling the human emotions

that have plagued me since birth

from the seeds of genomics…

Thought for once I was Pegasus

with the fervent wings, stained

with the undead blood of Medusa,

carrier of the ashes of the ancients

a myth, a belief, and nothing more…

The halo was overwhelming,

too caustic a pain for the heart

was the volcano underneath,

bursting with existential angst

searing every fibre within the man…

But then I became something else

unreal, not belonging to the bounds

of the trenches of the glorified wars

or the remnants of skeletal martyrs,

Not in the circles of tribalistic pride

or the vainglory of fenced territories

I was the outpouring of the volcano

that had buried the anger for long,

unleashing the primal fiery forces

on the absurd vanity of humanity!

I smelt peculiar, of burnt orange

a fruit that had sacrificed itself

in the fire of pain, to be painless

and free from the viciousness

of unbearable genetic entanglement…

The words flowed from the fruit-fly

as an advice and as a warning,

from the liberator of the orchard

the superhuman tracing its origins

from the book of the philosopher,

to demystify the parable of human life…

Untied from the bonds of the earth

to edge closer to the becoming

of a celestial being without aspirations

to fly and soar into the heights,

as I had become the sky myself

an illusion within the fragmented illusion

to seed the genus of *un-humans*

draped in the most ancient of sunshine…

AT THE CUSP OF A DAWN

A dawn

for the infinite beings

and for those ephemerals

confined to time…

a dawn

for the sun

to remind itself that it's a star

burning energy for mortals

trapped in a remote world…

a dawn

for the ever-flowing river

to change into crimson robes

without breaking the vow of silence…

a dawn

for the womb of darkness

to birth the light

to feed the famished lives

with invisible motherly hands…

a dawn

for the mind to awaken

after centuries of sleep

to seed the thoughts…

a dawn

for the dunes to reckon

they belong to the shore

cradled by the seas…

a dawn

for the boundless ocean

with unfathomable depths

mothering another world…

a dawn

for the living

and the parted souls

who belong elsewhere…

a dawn

for the carnivore

to fetch its unwitting prey

for the cycle of sustenance…

a dawn

for the timeless fig tree

to speed its wings of shade

for the vacant mendicant…

a dawn

for the blooms in the vase

to donate their fragrance

before withering away…

a dawn

for the prayers of goodness

propitiating the godliness

to banish the devilry…

a dawn

to keep the volcano asleep

and peaceful at heart

with no nightmare of an eruption…

a dawn

for the mountains

to deeply meditate

removed from worldly desires…

a dawn

for the hapless humans

and muted gods to ponder over

their earthly and heavenly lives…

a dawn

for the characters to enact

the incoherent script

to be staged in the world…

a dawn

for the scriptures

and the minds behind the words

who sought the meaning of life…

a dawn

for the fanciful myths

and the uncanny realities

to continue to enchant humanity…

a dawn

not just another one

but a novel chapter

that seems to be unread

with images speaking of familiarity

yet so distant in memory…

THE SLEEPING FLY

Who's in meditation

that phase of sleep

of the mortal eyes

when the mind is awake,

more awake than ever…

Is it the man at the table

seated with his arms crossed,

or the flowery teapot

within which is the warmth

for a wintry night?

Or, is it the fly

which hasn't got a name (as yet)

barely moving its antenna

as if it is listening keenly

to the murmurs of the mind,

the conversations of the man

with his own self,

whilst the tea within the pot

which like a stream

within a mythical ocean

talks in faint whispers…

The fly hears everything

every single beat of the heart

within the open room;

Symbolic of the soul

in the room of the universe,

where the dead speak

to the shadows of the living,

as verses of unrequited love

poignant with the remembrances

etched in the memories,

to be heard only in silence

and to be forgotten

like everything else,

as the mountain peaks melt

drifting slowly along the river

to reach the barren desert

within the mind of the man

where it would snow all night long,

to leave a single dew drop

on the withering rose petal

at the break of dawn…

A MAN WITH A MIND

What does a birthday signify?

Is it true or just another lie?

That a man is alive all the same

at this particular point in time…

On an unstoppable winning streak

heading to his destined peak

or being rattled in a trough

the climes being ruthlessly rough!

Chronologically, it is the anniversary

of the birth of a man who is wary

of what in reality lies ahead

what the oracles have left unsaid…

Passing the middle station of life

making some sense of the strife,

that many a fragrant thorn

awaits every man who has been born,

Like the fish inside a cube of glass

that does not know about its loss,

of the boundless freedom without pain

to swim in the vastness of the ocean,

Entrapped he is in the stubborn illusion

of a life that is relentlessly in motion,

with the happenings bringing forth

changes, masking the monuments of truth

left behind by the thoughtful ancients

who dug deep into the nuances,

unassuaged by the illusions of a world

that promised them with fool's gold!

The date reminds him of his journey

of a mysterious evolution from the tree,

learning as a primate to walk on all fours

then on two limbs, to fight against the woes

that brought to his eyes tears of despair

sensing the dread that was in the air;

The calmness harboured a storm

he was anxious about what was to come,

always living in fear of the future

and not trustful of the moods of nature,

he, with others, had to learn to stay together

to survive as a unit braving the weather!

The birthday reminds him of a strangeness

that resides within him, the aloneness

of a silent inner being, detached

that has left the window unlatched

to let in untrammelled the music of the soul

to flow into the lone caveman's hole

like a river touching the shores

of melancholy, unperturbed by the

downpours…

The day reminds him about one last thing

about the present state of being,

of being human, with the highs and lows,

the goodness and the inevitable flaws,

to continue to strive, to be true

to the self, not to be one among the few

but to be the only one, a man with a mind

on earth, to which the wandering soul does not bind…

THE DILUTION

Melancholy

isn't a shade of blue

but a white night

without rain or storm,

that has the musical notes

of a pensive Nature,

like a lady at the window

brooding over the timelessness

of her existence,

With a colourless attire

and no fire in her eyes,

the only sparkle in the room

being the reflection from

the solitary pearl

in her ear ring,

her stillness is a living memory

a horizontal moody line

an octave between the notes

that speaks of sadness,

An intriguing figurine

draped in silence, displaying

the illusion of perfection

and the impermanence

of everything in life

and its paraphernalia,

like exuberant youthful clouds

with the salt of life,

sailing with nonchalance

in the mortal blueness

of the summery skies,

swiftly and unconsciously

into the blank pages

of a wordless winter…

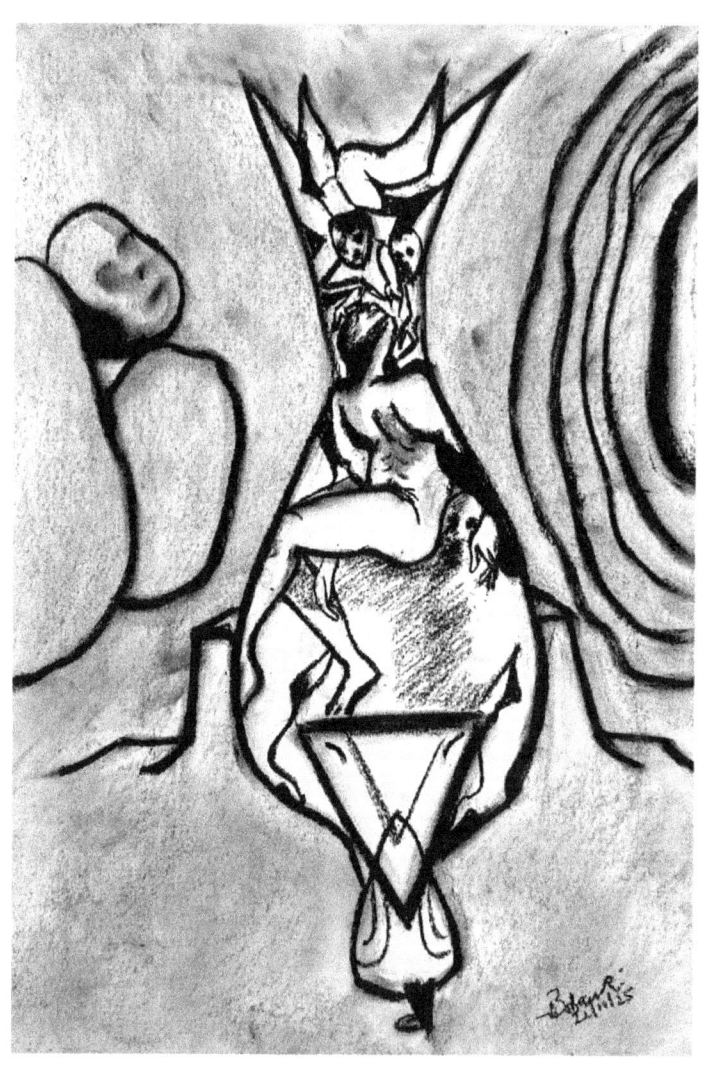

THE MUSIC IN THE VALLEY

More is conveyed

through monosyllables

than through words,

Silence is most profound

in the valley of solitude

where the sparrows

speak of human sorrows,

where the ancient river

journeys along its path

with memories of the old

and hopes of the new…

The strangeness that thus far

had kept the man away

from the springs of quietness

fades into the embracing fog,

heralding a new dawn…

The butterfly in the heart

flutters its imaginary wings

and begins to meditate,

synchronising with the mood

of contemplative dispassion

that impregnates the air…

If only man could forget

the vainly painful past

to follow the unperturbed course

of the flowing waters

reckoning the emptiness

that await everything,

If only he could remember

the ashes at the heart of the river

emptied from the urn of the dead

who once walked the earth

while and resplendent with life…

If only he could care to listen

to the song of the souls

shorn of the romantic beauty

but intensely poetic expressing

the eternal nature of the puzzle

that is called human life…

The tired and haggard traveller

could pause to reflect on the waters

that have relentlessly flown

since the ancient of times,

The figure staring back

from the mirror in the waters

with shadows of the lost souls

would remind him with kindness

and unearthly compassion,

the meaninglessness of the search

for a meaning in life...

GHOSTS OF INNOCENCE

What emerges from the carnage

is the dove draped in ashes

with cold bloodless eyes

and a serpentine tail of smoke,

wailing like unborn children

but tearless like their mothers

who aren't humans anymore,

but angels! in earthly paradise

where the dreams smell of flesh

young and full bodied burnt alive

for the demons with voids in hearts

to feast upon with their blind eyes!

With the blueness of the skies wiped

with the blood of innocence

slaughtered like sheep in the altar

of entrenched parochial hatred,

they aren't the skies where birds fly

to pronounce their boundless freedom

but a desolate space littered with

unmarked graveyards swarming with

the countless worms of hopes…

As people watch from a great distance

the *spectacle* in a distant land,

the tragedy is buried in silence,

though the violence is candid

with the fiends of visceral hatred

demolishing every tenet of humanity

and torching the funeral pyre of love,

on which the remnants of a civilisation

would be built upon, for posterity,

Those undead children of the future

who'll walk into the icy cold marble tomb

of a permanent pitch dark night…

THE CANOPY

Why did I think about the park today

I don't know for sure!

The place where it's all green

with nest-less birds and fidgety squirrels

the air with a fenestrated veil of serenity

close to the urban jungle, yet feeling remote

and thriving within the garb of silence

only occasionally broken by the cries

of an antique outdated animal

mistaking it for mysterious wilderness!

It must some form of a sanctuary

for the lost souls, this verdant place

that cannot forever stay lively and green…

Yet the bench that sits empty on its own

has a welcoming leafy shade above it,

for the character, masked and nameless,

to bear the harsh experience of life

not to get scalded by vain tears

or to be blinded in the fire of reality…

Every lonely pace entices the soul

as it requires peace as its only abode,

farther from the bitterness of existence

to couch on the grass of remoteness,

to quickly forget and to be quietly forgotten

as a weightless particle of little relevance,

slowly sinking in the music of quietude

where every grass blade and every flower

that cannot breathe the air freely anymore

amidst the clouds of withered leaves,

would eventually come to rest!

THE TRIAL

The eyes surveil

for fear to prevail

in the minds

of men of all kinds!

That's how freedom

is stolen from them,

so that they won't think

and through paper and ink

mount a rebellion

against the dominion…

With freedom lost

democracy is a ghost,

With intellect sent to exile

people become servile

to the vicious cycle of fear,

as they breathe the unfree air…

They fear the trial

the lengthy ordeal

though they've committed no crime

but found guilty all the same!

Fear is what rules over them

as there plays the requiem

at the funeral of freedom

to be buried without a brainstorm…

THE BURGLAR

The cunning burglar

who accidentally steps into

the anonymous poet's lair

too is doomed to be a poet!

Like the mice and the flies

the tailless lizards and the ants

like every nondescript form of life

entrapped within those walls,

he too would recite verses

that erupt from the volcano

masquerading as a tallow candle

in the pernicious darkness…

He would no longer feel joy

but a perceptible sadness,

the inevitable pain of thought

would invade his hardened heart

and render it insane enough

to realise the precariousness

of his existence as a human…

He would find the world

a mysterious deep forest

abandoned by the gods

and dwelled by innumerable people

who are no longer humans

but demons in disguise!

He would feel unwanted

by a world obsessed with life,

like the unconventional words

bound to the ivies on the walls

not transmitted anywhere, but

just keep echoing back to his soul…

Who has been here before, he wonders

the space shallow like a den

must have a story, a verse about itself

unsaid by the man who was here,

a living being who was human

a poet, one with a heart

that could palpate sorrow

and one which blazed with indignation

at the plight of the species of the wise!

His heart must have bled to death

as it could no longer bear the pain

of the human indifference to suffering…

What makes me think about others

Is it the man who lived here

in this parallel universe of his own,

challenging the sacrosanct morals

and the futility of worship

of a world that dehumanised others

into subservience and slavery?

How do *I* know

the intricacies of *his* thoughts,

the melancholy of his aggrieved mind

and the words stemming from his heart?

Is he alive, in this dark space

perhaps as a soul, as they say

bewitching everyone who comes this way

like the cunning of a burglar

sneaking into their gullible minds

and feeding them with his own thoughts!

The lair teems with lives

of all forms, with no barrier,

everything here has its own mind

parroting the words of the man

who was once ignored by all!

It is always night in here

the candle exudes bright light

welcoming the travellers of all ilk,

The dead poet's humble abode

has become a repository of words,

woven into precise verses

for both animals and men to chant

like nursery rhymes

deep in the underground!

KAFKA'S MOMENT

Kafka,

when he would introspect

often found himself as an insect

not even a giant beetle

but one too thin and little,

who was deeply insecure inside

and his frame feeble from outside;

That he was inconspicuous

he was all too conscious,

An irrelevant bug on the wall

but that which had a soul

that yearned to document its plight

showing human life in a new light

to the sanguine world

about existential crisis untold...

But how in words could he write

the profoundness of his insight,

the sheer volume of melancholic anxiety

the sadness that overshadowed gaiety?

Wouldn't it be apathetic to vocalise

the truth, that life was but a pack of lies?
Empty papers beckoned him from the desk
but writing was an insurmountable task
to the writer, who would procrastinate
unable to open that lichened gate
that would lead to the unspoilt path
of self-revelation, to take the solemn oath
to be truly honest to one's own thought
and to ink what the self has taught…
Days and nights vainly passed by
and Kafka would let out a sigh
over the yet not spoken or written words
as if they were trapped in his vocal cords!
The candies helplessly burned away
and the writer in him would cry and pray
for serendipity, for that *one* moment
when destiny would reveal its intent!
It was naturally bound to happen
that he would find the missing ink in his pen
when he chanced to met *Felice*
the vision that lifted him out of the abyss,
that compelled him to form his *judgement*
and tell the world aloud what life really meant…

THE MAN-CHILD ON THE SHORE

Life is...

what?

a *knowing* drop of ocean

in a child's innocent hand?

or the *unknowable* sand

clutching on the feet of man?

The memories of bonds

alive in flesh and fresh blood

is juxtaposed with

the clotted images of those gone,

Are they the catalysts

for man to continue his hopeful pursuit

to alchemise his drifting dreams?

The ocean that harbours

a universe underneath the waves,

knows better than the man

who dreams from the land!

It's all about *knowing*

what's behind the superfluous

the gossamer of emotions

that masks the truth…

The shadows seldom speak

to the *deaf* ears of man!

But they converse with the soul

in the pristine language of silence

that has no dialects or semantics…

Is there space beyond what is seen

through the technological eyes?

Why do the stars have the wondrous charm

whilst one knows they're dead?

Why this relentless disturbance

the tremors within the mind

not satiated by the facades of modernity?

Why did man belittle love as a crop

to be harvested with the desirous sickle

to suit his dissolute lifestyle?

Does civilisation hold anymore meaning

when love is traded as a commodity?

What is he?

a speck in the society

or a society in himself,

a whole world of unspoken words

and unexpressed thoughts?

Like the fossil searching for its lost story

man yearns to know more,

knowing well the answers are opaque

and guarded by the doors of time…

BETRAYAL

Democracy is our forefathers'

thoughtful gift to humanity,

So is the freedom of ours

of all citizens, noble and laity

regardless of birth, caste, race,

the fruit of their selfless sacrifice…

In angst many a night they hadn't slept

But the promises they have kept

for the betterment of the morrows

when they put their lives down in the gallows…

The fundamental idea of society

we inherited from the minds of antiquity,

That is the intellectual property

of the people, the collective, for posterity,

Not to be vouchsafed by the rulers

but to be cherished by the entire masses!

They who from the scratch built the nation

had set the wings of reforms in motion,

to propel the fledgling towards progress

battling the scourge of social distress;

A tall beacon of unrelenting hope

for successive generations not to stop

in their pursuit of healing the divisions

to accommodate people of all visions…

We've betrayed the forebears

coldly, callously as if nobody cares!

We've even intoxicated the successors

with racial poison, the humanity's curse!

Dark is the future, hostile is the political weather

but we think, we act sensibly, we wouldn't dither!

THE DOOR IN THE WOODS

At the wooden door is the forest

the uninvited esteemed guest!

with its myriad teeming lives

gone silent, with whispering cries…

Under the blue satiny moonlight

like the guardian of the night,

with sprites perched on trees

glistening in the shadowy hues

of soulful cuckoos and sparrows

blanketed in the ancient moss!

The door creaks open to let inside

the leafy giants and their pride

unleashed from the wilderness

to the cave of silence, to regress

into the mythical human form

multi limbed with magical eyes!

They swarm into the white bed like bugs

crawling to the skull through the legs,

The eggs on the cypresses hatch

and baby angels toddle along the patch

of moist green on their mother's breasts

as the moon crowns the mount's crest…

The forest that is a world of dreams

merges with the house without seams,

with all its families of fauna and flora

transformed into a human aura;

With the melted candles gone cold

and the purple irises no longer bold,

moths escape from the forest's angel eyes

along with the innocent household mice

and the absentminded resident soul

and the infinitely meditative night owl,

to live and die in imperfect peace

to live and die in torpid peace…

AN ABSENT PICTURE

I graze over the barren walls

Full of identical bricks

clothed with a neutral shade

that lacks any clear identity!

I imagine a picture hanging there

at the corner on my left

as my right ear gets drilled,

A picture that hasn't

the flamboyance of colours

or dynamism of human figures,

but vocal through its silence…

I sink into an open eyed dream

where the imagery has spread

like ink diffusing itself

all through the walls!

The space is more silent

than it has ever been before

speaking volumes about finding identity

through the prisms of art…

The clinic room has become

a thoughtful work of poetic beauty

shedding its nervous objectivity

and opening its eyes to the world

like a flower reaching out to the sun…

I know the walls will be blank

neat and tidy and unemotional,

in the face of callous reality!

But I prefer to hold on to the illusion

that they are dreaming about art

to fill their vacant minds…

I admit that I prefer to believe

that the walls too have eyes

that yearn for the stars!

THE WINTER OF YOUTH

I got it wrong

How could I be fooled

all along, I wonder!

The album I was browsing

with such casual confidence

was in the reverse order!

The past was the present

and vice versa,

apparently to my eyes,

trained so thoroughly

by nearly half a century of life!

I must have been younger

in those days begone,

At least the timelines say so

though they don't scream out

of the stained screen

brooding over in silence instead…

I think about perception

its beauty and its fallibility,

The wall clock reminds me

of the concept of punctuality,

It could be a myth

An illusion of optics amongst others,

like the colours of the skies

and the autumn leaves,

all so vibrant before fading away…

What if man wakes up

in a timeless zone somewhere surreal

remembering only the future,

with no memory of the past?

The collection of tales of the present

is vulnerable to be erased,

leaving one not with a blank slate

but a richness of future visions

and an experience of life

in another sensory format

that he would come to regard as real…

He wouldn't think

that he has got it wrong,

he is one petal that has fallen off

from the sunflower dial of the clock

finding its own thinking space,

levitating in a heaven-less dream!

True, the appearance has changed

the wrinkles are conspicuous

and the narrow paths on the facial muscles

littered with pigments inked by time;

The cells are ageing, relentlessly

processing the matter and energy

to keep the fire alive

within the confines of finitude,

till the run ends in some way or other

without a definitive destination;

It is a genetic marathon

the baton passed on to posterity

as the forebears watch from the galleries,

faceless but perceptive…

The mist is vocal

about stories of people buried

in the catacombs of time,

who calculated every second of their life

but still got it all wrong in the end!

Between the extremes of joy

and the deep pits of sadness,

they had a life to live,

a day to look forward to

and a night to rest their souls…

Like the Mount Vesuvius spewing fire

turning Pompeii into frozen ashes,

the stability in life is uprooted

when land suddenly becomes water

and man is thrown to the shores

as a hapless fish

left to the mercy of time…

To become an amphibian

which could survive the ordeal

would be his only wish,

his heartfelt prayer to the gods,

if he still had a heart

and if he still believed in any god…

A FISH-FLY

My past was a fish

and my future is a fly

In the present time

I'm a man,

in a flux of states

between a fish and a fly!

When will I realise

that I'm only an animal

happening to be here

who is cloaked in morals

and trapped as a picture

within the archives of time?

Within the rationality of science,

the abstraction of philosophy

and the beauteous wings of poetry

is a soul that seeks the truth,

Truth that would set one free

bringing him closer to the reality

that the essence of life is in the art,

the expression of another dimension

inconspicuous to naked eyes!

What millions of lives of the fish

and millions of lives of the fly

didn't suffice to realise,

man can hope to find

in a single human birth…

ICY

It's cold outside

the tiles feel like ice

not thawed after the night,

As the quiet wind moves

the sleepy shrubs in the yard,

the coffee mug shivers

the concoction no longer warm

not worth sipping anymore!

But the moment exists

so do I…

in this bubble of mid-winter

when the lavenders stand still

whilst the burrows are active

with creatures in hibernation,

sleeping through their warm dreams!

It is a long way to go

into the iridescent starry night

when the sprites will come to play

behind the firs and pines

in their natural habitat!

The fragmented moment of winter

eager to evanesce into the dusk

fascinated with the brilliant colours

but aware of the end in darkness,

as one amongst the transient stars

augmenting the silence of the skies…

I think about the rotten trench

the open grave in wintry wilderness

for the young half dead soldier,

where the moribund burned with fever

amongst the decaying corpses

as the war-cries faded at a distance…

He must have thought about love

for his mother,

his fledgling romance

with his heartthrob,

the boy's attachment to his bicycle

and the fragrance of yellow roses

in the garden at home

that belonged to a beautiful dream,

within the mortifying nightmare of reality…

Peace was forced to be frozen
hardened than the harshest of winter,
Love was a liability, a weakness
unbecoming of a strong man,
In the trench would be buried
his deeper cache of thoughts
the pencil scribbles on love and hope,
and his rigid body paraded
as an effigy of a martyr,
who bravely laid down his life
for his fatherland…
As men with their conscience dead
walk the earth with carefree abandon
the soldier's soul sinks into the abyss
where stars go to die forever,
along with the refugees perishing
on the long marches
through hatred in frozen mindsets
in their battles for survival;
The night would be bleakly starless
once the souls lose their faith
in the hibernating minds of the living
and the vestiges of humanity on earth…

THE LAND

The strange terrain

to be meandered through,

that has in its deeper shelves

the layers of evolving civilisations

with the bony vestiges of the past

the monuments of sacrifices of yore,

where the prophetesses' oracles

of the future once reverberated,

that has at the core of its heart

the seeds of a violent earthquake

and the impassive raw rocks of peace,

The qualia of benign and malignant

shades in the transient moods of nature,

The philosophy of art and poetry

and the transcendental vibrations of music

that hold the answers to the human plight

and the keys to the windows of the universe

is your own self, within your soul!

The promised land within you

sans the aura of supernaturalism

and the temptations of immortality,

is the space that belongs only to man

occupied by his beastly fear of death

and the mournful staring eyes of reality;

The land that hides no pots of gold

but has the panacea for the human pains

that awaits exploration by naked hands

without the exasperating burden of hopes

and without the sadness of despair!

HOLE IN THE SKULL

The slithery snake too has

delicate designs on its skin

speckled dots in colours

with true aesthetic appeal

that would cleverly camouflage

its deeper venomous instincts!

So too are men on the surface

with their impermeable faces

that cannot be read!

Under the social mask

is concealed a sardonic grin

like that of an awake cadaver!

The real devil, they say, is honest

in his vile intentions

without the garb of morals!

The cunning would deceive

with their sophistications

while proud of preying on gullibility!

Demons are born human

and not chiseled out of boulders,

cocooned in the wombs of mothers

to be nurtured as children,

who knew how to play and laugh

and make the best of their lives!

The abstraction of the psyche

brings forth suspicion and hatred,

Like clouds shrouding the skies

the youthful minds filled with spite,

learn the skill of hiding through words

the truly abominable face of evil…

Those ones who cannot get enough

of their perfectly curated images,

are blind to the plight of the world;

They thrive in the misery of others

and pretend to be their saviours

staunchly believing in their own falsity!

Insanity is not murderous

but, remember, the devil is often sane!

With full cognisance of the acts

of violence and bloodshed

with devastating consequences,

the devil carries out his pogrom…

Trust the honest devil

for he doesn't hide his crimes,

But as for the perfidious part-human

one can't say what he is up to,

for, hatred sugarcoated with love

is sweeter to the unsuspecting palate!

The snake coiled inside the skull

aching to spew the venom

is subservient to the predator

who buries his pathological psyche

within the cloak of goodness

Readying himself to strike at his leisure!

RABID

Violence is *natural*

The cloudless skies speak

volumes about the rains,

The melodious breeze

Is a storm in disguise!

The foetus to be born

will be bathed in blood,

The (fear of) upcoming events,

the haphazard happenings

that have no logic or pattern

baffle the sane minds

instigating self-suspicion

and a credence

that violence is inevitable,

inherent in nature

and all the lives within her…

Silence is profound

the extreme of violence,

Without any blood spill

or hint of a twist

is the calmness

that is strangely foreboding…

If only the fallen blooms

could voice their hearts aloud

about the violence

of the breeze or the raindrops!

Peace is the ultimate goal

to be strived for

but it is not the state of the living

who are in perpetual fear

of the spillover of violence

happening within themselves!

The incessant inner turmoil

is the greatest of wars in itself

that is answerable to no courts of law,

The storm follows no rules

devastating and transforming life

in its attack of insanity…

Pacifism is a belief

not written in stone

that needs no reasoning,

An armour against injury

from the traumas of life,

a lantern's light of optimism

in a world that cares for none

and is obsessed with the chaos

of senseless derailed minds…

THE MEMORIES OF A DREAM

The characters levitate

defying the physical laws

and walk in thin air

in space, above the ground

yet they're rooted in the heart

like the figures in a painting

so rich in vitality and alive,

but not exactly so, (to the conscious)

as they don't see me, the beholder

who is lost in that vision,

Where the ghosts talk

their eyes with white reflexes

still covey their *absent* minds…

They are still lives

with an illusive dynamism

that's profoundly real

which captivates the eyes

and entraps the viewer

into a neatly woven web of belief;

The images flow like a river

that is gently following the course

unhurried about reaching anywhere!

I see my friends, hear their voices

sometimes aimlessly maundering

coherent at other times

amongst a crowd of people

including children in school uniforms

in a vibrant atmosphere

simulating a carnival with activities!

I have never seen these people

and I won't meet them again,

But they aren't lifeless dolls,

They're real, like any other

citizens of the dreamy world!

I felt ecstatic at a painting

within the painted dream,

it was yellow and green

with life sized human figures,

The art is here to stay

I tell myself, with an exulted heart!

People walk past, it is night time

They queue up for more events

incessantly chatting and shuttling

between the lit up tents,

with spectacular joys in store!

Like every dream

there is no beginning or end

just the middle segment, the present

this one is no different

The crowd must have melted away

or they may still be there, in space

suspended from the other reality

leaving the viewer with etchings,

random scribbles on paper

folded within an envelope

titled:

The memories of a dream!

TIME TRAP

Time is not lost

or gained, says the wise!

Prophecy is not for the future

it is essentially timeless

and not bound by covenants;

The past is only a perception

that belongs to the realm

of dreams and fantasies…

The world is created

within the eyes of the man

moulded in his perceptions,

who wakes up from his dream

to eerily familiar imagery

which he ought to accept as real

and amicable to his mind;

Whilst that world is strange

not even remotely familiar

to the others around him,

Not even his bosom friends

who live in the same space

and breathe the same air

recognise that as theirs,

living in parallel worlds

defined by their own minds…

That vacant churchyard

where one runs into

on a stormy evening,

only to realise the immensity

of the engulfing loneliness,

where the only signs of life

are the vague footprints

partly obliterated by rains,

is the world that is inhabited

only by the self…

Man is dual hearted

an intricate brainy one

and an emotional other

contrasting the singular life

that dwells in its own world…

Like the volcano metamorphosing

into a meditative mountain

after venting its anger,

the individual's world changes

into something else to which he has to adapt himself

like a mouse within a trap

knowingly savouring the snack

bit by bit, to the last bite

that fate has set up for it

with unusual kindness…

The lost time

that is desperately searched for

by every man who walked the earth

is a void, a hole

in which emptiness thrives;

The phantoms of loss

would still remain at large

as a misperception

even after the trap door

has closed with a finality

over which man doesn't have a say!

The bells toll at night

reverberating through the churchyard

as shadows walk along the walls

in search of the lost…

AHEAD IN BELIEF

The world is not poor in belief

for, who wouldn't want *moksha*

the holy waters to wash off their sins

and a paradise to look after after-life

where the life becomes a seed again,

a human being with a definitive identity

translated into one of the countless atoms

to be reborn or released from the cycle

of life and death on the mystery planet!

It is a rich thought, that vitalises life

An unprovable idea about an invisible soul

A befitting conclusion to the human tale

that there are *happenings* in the aftermath

of living, where the life is scrutinised

from the beginning of the chapter to the end

and the epilogue is scripted by an entity

who has masterly control over the universe…

That is a fertile and portent imagination

borne out of the deepest meditation

of the ancestors who walked this earth,

mystified by the human condition

and mortified by the reality of end to life,

unsure about their precarious existence

whether it was any different to animals

or it was a sarcastic pastime of the gods!

Their belief was their answer to nature

to defy the rules of the destructive forces,

creating images with supernatural powers

whose massive wings were powerful enough

to transcend into the world of immortality…

As men prospered, so did their beliefs

the scattered units of thoughts unified

into sacrosanct volumes for posterity;

Faith was the symbol of human resistance

the determination not to succumb

to the time-bound inevitability of death,

to go past that into the realm of after-death

where the soul finally found its meaning,

and an answer to the question of life

centred around the sadness of tragedy…

Faith is a skilfully engineered tool

that explores the anxieties and fears

that inhabit the recesses of the mind…

It is a reassurance of positivity

which however false it maybe, is comforting

a guide for the mysterious journey in life,

through the complexities and inadequacies;

It should be no wonder that modernity

is inclined to believe in the occult,

as the times are insecure and hazardous,

with the quest for immunity from mortality

still searching for answers in the dark;

Man doesn't feel he is the master of his soul

and is unwilling to yield to failures,

He hopes to alchemize the elixir of life

that would dispel the gnawing innate fears

and shut the doors on death forever,

attaining the unshakeable permanence

that he had always aspired for

and to do away with the gods and myths!

MONOCHROME

Bones are white

so must be the soul

contrasting with the darkness

that fills the dead eyes…

Thoughts are white

papers with cryptic scribbles

later translating into words

in the crate of silence…

The day is white

dotted with luminescent greens

along the shore of the lake

in a peaceful state of arrest…

The night is white

to the insomniac author

In quietude the brittle words calcify

into meaningful passages

of love, despair and hope…

The forest is white

the imaginary fairies draped in fog

holding their wands of magic

in the desolate wild space…

With such withies of images

from a scattered dream

where a tidal wave of fever

seizes the unconscious dreamer,

the monochrome takes shape

nurtured by the placental blood

in the cave within the mind…

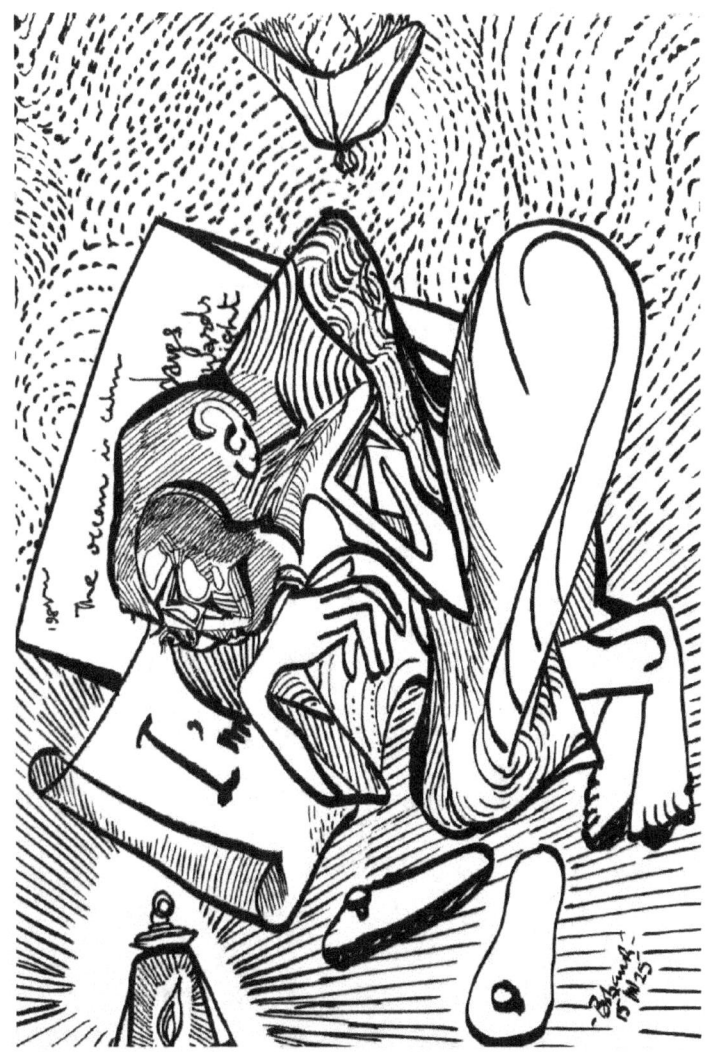

THROUGH THE HALF-OPEN DOOR

When sound enters the corridor

it realised that the ear has a lock

on its door, on the right

The mystified sound looks to the left

but it too has one, half-locked!

One should be reminded that

there are only two doors,

Through the half-open left door

the sound half-enters with trepidation,

There're still the breezy whispers of leaves

or a naked poet sauntering on the grass,

giving one the enchanting visuals

of a solemn autumn evening…

His corridor is seen at a distance

and he hopes in all earnest

that he is isn't locked out of both rooms.

when he eventually makes it there!

The seas are spuriously calm

with the silhouette of a half sunk ship

that still has some life left at the stern,

a monument, an augury of the what lies next!

The half-open door welcomes

the sounds to enter and leave images

of the world, for the mind to see,

The corridor has the memories of footfalls

of sounds that couldn't realise their sensory potential,

But nothing would unbolt the right door

that meditates in its innocent blankness,

Unaware of the calamitous waters out there

picking up odd tones, like someone maundering

over the plain shadows of silence…

GHOST IN THE BOX

The night communicates in many ways

but the most through its gaze,

I still remember like yesterday

a night that goes back a long way,

I watched an episode of a series in the box

after the mundane telecast of political talks!

Someone had died in that story in his youth

An apparition that couldn't open its mouth

is what he became, that poor young man

I believe he followed the lady down the lane

without her knowing that she had a shadow

that was not hers! It rains that night

and outside the window there is that sight,

staring back from under the only street lamp

Through the vertical water curtains

came that gaze, with the deepest of pains,

but frightening all the same!

To my mind stuck forever that frame,

I remember looking out through the glass

my heart thumping and my mind at a loss,

only to see the space under the street light

to reassure myself it was empty like the night!

But a ghost could be transparent, invisible

standing by the bedside, fixing his stare on the gullible!

That night I crossed myself as I went to bed

telling myself if he turns up, I will just play dead!

He didn't, for he was just an actor playing the role

But his gaze had something that pierced the soul

that has firmly adhered to me ever since

But why? Some things in life don't make any sense!

A MATTER OF DISTINCTION

The extraterrestrial

won't have a clue about art

or about poetry,

Perhaps too prosaic

lacking wit and charm,

Everything that makes one human

would be absent in "it,"

For want of love

or out of simple curiosity

even if "it" were to come here,

There would be nothing in common

except the physiognomy…

Too straight will be its thoughts

with no hint of abstraction,

No thoughts reflecting

from the river of a symphony,

or an intriguing disturbance

stemming from a painting,

No insight or afterthoughts

would illuminate "it,"

It would be compelled to leave

due to lack of that finer sense

of aesthetics, of beauty, of art…

Science wouldn't distinguish

between the extraterrestrial and man,

Art, and only art would

give man that soul that is entirely his!

UNDER THE CRIMSON SKIES

The sands know the crowd

gathering on holidays

to savour the crimson evening,

when after a hot day,

the radiant sun departs

like a mystic sinking into meditation…

"Rejoice! The night is about to be born"

sang the poet, in his mind!

"Alas! The day has died

the skies are red faced with grief!"

muttered the philosopher

"The earth is moving

with the onward journey of time!"

asserted the scientific mind

"Here on earth today

Gone tomorrow, to his creator!"

said the religious one

"The return of the sun at dawn

is at the root of all human hopes!"

claimed another, carried away

by the profoundness of his own discovery!

"The sun doesn't set

except in the eyes of the living!"

was yet another personal opinion;

The sight of the distant redness

was comforting for many city folks

who, caught up in the web of anxiety

sought a breathing space to relax!

There were survivalists amongst them

who were sceptical about the sun,

that the dawn may never return

and it would all be darkness!

Away from the sadness

of romantic break ups

deaths and burials

and poetic wistful longings,

Away from the scientific sensibility

of the law of colours, geometry

and the physics of nature,

Away from the stairs of time

and the mysterious heavens

wrapped within flimsy clouds,

Away from the fascinating science

and the sharpness of reason,

Away from poetry and philosophy

of serendipity and inevitability,

the beauty of love and the tragedy of death,

the apprehensions about the future

and the haunting phantoms of the past,

Children played on the shores

that belonged only to them

untouched by the worldly anxieties,

for they were there only to play

and nothing else really mattered in the world…

THE JUXTAPOSED MIRRORS

What brings people closer

is the magnetism of food,

What strings them together

is the thread of thoughts,

A bunch of wandering nomads

settled around a wild grain field

to form a singular society,

the first of many to follow

where people shared ideas

for common good,

rather than sole individual survival;

Faith was still embryonic

rooted in the primal fear

of the forces of nature,

Brotherhood is instinctive

a humane project creating a bulwark

against the invasion by elements…

Humans living in isolation

symbolically parted by fences

but curious about each other's plight

tell their strange but poignant stories

gathering around the warmth

of a decorated tea pot,

digesting the bitter afterthoughts

under the half-dawned moon…

With their belief long gone

and their own selves challenged

by the countless years of solitude,

They strive to grapple with

the cold face of their reality,

of being lost in a cosmic isle

with the warmth of a friendship

budding like a blue lotus

in the placid waters of the soul…

THE UNDERGROUND MAN

Out there is a slippery world

where the minds have gone cold,

numbed by limitless digital parodies

the twisted stories that give them highs!

It is the era of political correctness

in everything from words to dress,

Man is not allowed to be man anymore

the moral scrutiny more than ever before,

forcing his true self to go underground

and wear the mask he has newly found!

His long legacy is judged by the crowd

who claim to be modern and empowered,

They're so damn perfect that they don't err

They would punish him even for a slur!

Truth is what they say is the truth

Every new age man is a moral sleuth

digging deep into other's words

and imposing sanctions on the vocal cords!

"Verbal whiplashes for the nonconformity"

Idols are thrashed with pompous gaiety

and paraded nude to be publicly stoned!

Their works are ridiculed and disowned

just because they aren't overly modern

and from the youth the old apparently failed to learn!

One simple misstep and that's all it takes

to be ditched in social media earthquakes,

To be mercilessly vilified and forgotten…

The underground man trusts his iron mask

to save him from being trampled over like husk!

WHAT THE RAVEN DOESN'T KNOW

The so-called average man

is deeply superstitious,

about almost everything!

He firmly believes in the omens

of the restless black cat

the music of the lizard on the roof

and even the hungry raven!

The night belongs to the witches

crafty in their ancient magic,

and the faceless homeless ghosts

who've no bodies to live in!

Insanity is possession, he says

by the godless devil,

who can be forcibly driven out!

The waters are "purely" polluted

but could redeem him from his sins!

The river where entire shoals of fish

have been poisoned to death

is supposed to give him immortality!

He's suspicious about shadows

and the foreboding darkness in itself,

that harbours the unforeseeable!

Every moment demands caution

to be vigilant against unknown predators

behind the trees or the bushes!

His forefathers never really die

but lurk in the recesses of the cosmos

eternally thirsty for salvation

and it is his duty to please them…

His entire life is carefully built

around a ritual concept of purity,

blissfully unaware that he is home

to countless germs within his own body!

Everything is by design

the happenings do not just happen

but have been so willed by the entity

that he trusts with his own life!

Science surely intrigues him

But faith pleases him the most,

which seals the voids with darkness

and straightens out a complex human life

into a simplistic tale of the body and soul!

Body for the worms or electric fires

and the imperishable soul for the heavens,

That's his theory of life,

that keeps his innate fear at bay

and anything that contradicts his views

would make him unsettled and suspicious,

he would poke the body of dense darkness

with his flameless lantern of superstitions!

ANTIDOTE

In the war ravaged zone

only staying alive matters

and, of course, death

the scores, headcount, tables

of the numbers of scalps…

But to the hapless one

who luckily misses the missile

and runs on limping legs

from the charred remains

with his clothes on fire,

unable to think for a moment

unable to grieve for the lost ones,

only staying alive counts,

all the rest is insignificant!

Maybe he has an incurable tumour

a dreadful malady of the cells,

that would kill him slowly

but surely, and he knows that too…

Yet, even while writhing in pain

he would spend the last fibre of energy

to conserve what is left

of his own life!

It is the intense attachment of man

to the precious experience

of being alive,

just breathing and being alive

bearing all the pain and the scars

the flashbacks of misery and bloodshed,

It is that undefinable bond

that man has forged with his life,

despite all the absurdities of the world,

That is how he counters the reality of death,

making him dream of immortality…

EPILOGUE OF A EULOGY

The corpse that sees no tears

or hears the praising eulogies,

gets a standing ovation

from the thronging crowd!

He is paid the last respects

as if to mask the regrets

of having excluded him

while he was alive and breathing!

He who is no longer a human life

is believed to belong to eternity,

he has crossed the long bridge

to the boundless unknown

and whilst he is given a farewell

as the body draped in flowers

is fed to the soil or the fire,

the assembled people seek immunity

from the fear of their own mortality…

They depart from the graveyard

momentarily forgetting their shadows

that would remind them of death,

that their time too would come to pass…

The stationary inanimate objects,

even the momentarily standstill atmosphere

would unleash suspicion in their minds,

with flashes of memories of the dead man

who was neatly dressed and perfumed

and with an ambiguous vigour on his face,

appeared to be deeply meditating…

The day of remembrance is not a single day

but virtually everyday of the year,

when the mourners when on their own

have to confront their own thoughts

that disturb their peace of mind…

The departed too had dreams unfulfilled

like every other human being on earth,

But the soul is totally indifferent, they say,

as it has nothing to do with the world anymore…

Yet, deep within, they see their own dreams

reflecting from the thoughts about the man

who, though dead, remains alive through memories…

Like a sleeping man attempting the past exams

of his childhood, through his dreams,

unable to comprehend the subjects

and the fear of failure looming over him,

immortality would remain evasive,

the unattainable that lures the subconscious

but keeps the flames of desire alive…

ODE TO THE SCARS

Scarred is every life

that lives on earth,

the umbilicus being the first

reminder of human pain…

Every moment leaves its mark

though only a few are indelible,

The invisible body of the mind

is a repository of scars

Every dream has a footprint

a scar, that is an afterthought,

Thinking has its own share of pain

wounding is the sharpness of truth

Grief is unyielding, joys are sparse

the satiety transient, the hunger is real

Humans are bound to grow up

to suffer in the name of bold maturity

They're only allowed the little freedom

to reminisce about their lost childhood

to grieve in the subconscious sphere

within the ambit of their dreams…

Life is often silent in its violence

traumatising everything in its path!

It has spared none who has been born

the pain endured with tactical survival

He realises that the world is a disaster

that it has no order or a dutiful master,

and that this is probably a transit point

where souls of strangers happen to meet…

That brings one to the farthest edge of loneliness

the acuteness of despair hard to describe

and though the pain eventually settles

the scar is bound to be there forever…

It all stems from within, man tells himself

but that offers him no consolation,

as that is an admission of his aloneness

in a place to which he is bounded by emotions…

Love, dreams, art, he has seen them all

unable to decipher what they intend to convey,

If life after all is a conversation with the self

what's the purpose of human bonds?

The trees that feed him with fruits

would simply die without food or water,

It could be that man is here as a gardener

to tend to the wounded souls around him,

which would keep his own mind sane

and the scars sealed without bleeding anymore…

The world of pain welcomes nobody

though most are here as invited guests,

Entrapped in the endless drought

humans are thirsty for a drop of love!

They come to believe this is a respite

sheltering them from something sinister

that could have been infinitely worser!

They desperately wait for a divine oracle

when in truth there is only one wisdom

that being the voice of the mind…

Every human has an element of mysticism

borne out of the pain from his own scars…

Life makes one realise the ground

and the unfriendliness of the terrains

that his forefathers once camped upon

through the climes to brazen it out…

In reality, nature belongs to none

and humans are here for their own sake,

Once the foetus becomes a newborn

he has no option but to live…

To fight back and be resilient,

to dream of peace when engulfed by wars

to find music within the dissonance

and an odd sense of beauty within the chaos…

AUTUMN MORNING

Autumn is a festivity

of colours,

rich and flamboyant

on one side

dead and decaying

on the other...

Thus thought Pissaro

as he mounted his canvas

in Eragny one morning...

It was breezy and cool

as the clouds opened

the blue shutters in the sky,

The rains stuttered

the fields were verdant

whilst the trees of all ilk

dressed in myriad colours,

the leaves ageing

and about to fly away

along with the gold crest

restlessly perched on a branch!

This is the time,

there may not be another

to capture the pensive mood

of the wet season,

in all its varying shades

of glory and fallibility,

in the mystic imagery

symbolic of life and death…

A man in solitude

wandering along the pastures

came to his mind,

But the character

living within the painted image

could well be in company

of the whispering leaves

telling their own stories!

What else has man got

apart from the philosophy

that he has extracted

from the veritable book of nature?

The transience is salient

as the clouds coalesce in silence

auguring a morning rain,

that would force the artist

to fold his possessions

and to seek shelter in the barn

with the rams and ewes

that know not what art is!

More often than not, he felt

that the truth of life

was just in living,

in being a beholder

delighted at the beauty of

the mesmerising work of art

that nature is…

AT THE CORE

If everything turns into dust

and die every man must,

from where does one get his will

to keep climbing steeply uphill?

The souls talk to him in silence

to help him make some sense

of the chaos and the absurdity

within human life's brevity;

He belongs to the ancients

his seed was their prescience,

His life might be here on lease

but he has been in the making for centuries!

What guided them through the night

was it their dreams or the hope of daylight?

Whatever happened to their dreams,

their resilience birthed the streams

flowing into the massive sea of humanity,

with creatures of intellect and beauty…

The dream of a swift transition

from deep darkness to a radiant dawn,

The insight into the impermanence

that makes profound the living experience

adds gravitas to his strifes

and infinite meaning to the many lives

that he leads here within the limited space,

and that earthly life is but one phase

amongst several others to come

though he knows not where from…

ONE AMONG OTHERS

It is good to remind oneself

That you're surrounded by animals,

beasts domesticated within the society,

untamed in the freedom of the forests,

and more importantly the bipeds,

that you should never dare to forget,

the most intelligent of all animals:

MAN!

The thinking animal, that has desires,

an insatiable lust for flesh and blood

hidden within his cave-like eyes,

The only creature who is conditioned

socially, to tame his own intellect,

just so that he wouldn't rationalise

and would be submissive to

CONTROL!

The species that has destabilised

and stripped nature to the bone,

has created a rigid hierarchy

in the name of maintaining order,

disenfranchising and dehumanising

his own brethren, erecting his culture

on the tears and ashes of the oppressed…

the unkind MANKIND!

Whoever departs from the norm

is deemed to be an eccentric figure,

Whoever criticises the established order

is stamped as insane to be feared,

The human world thrives in absurdities

that contradict its own accomplishments,

It is good to remind oneself time and again

that you're one amongst them,

one among the many MEN on the planet,

the unreasonable who seeks reason!

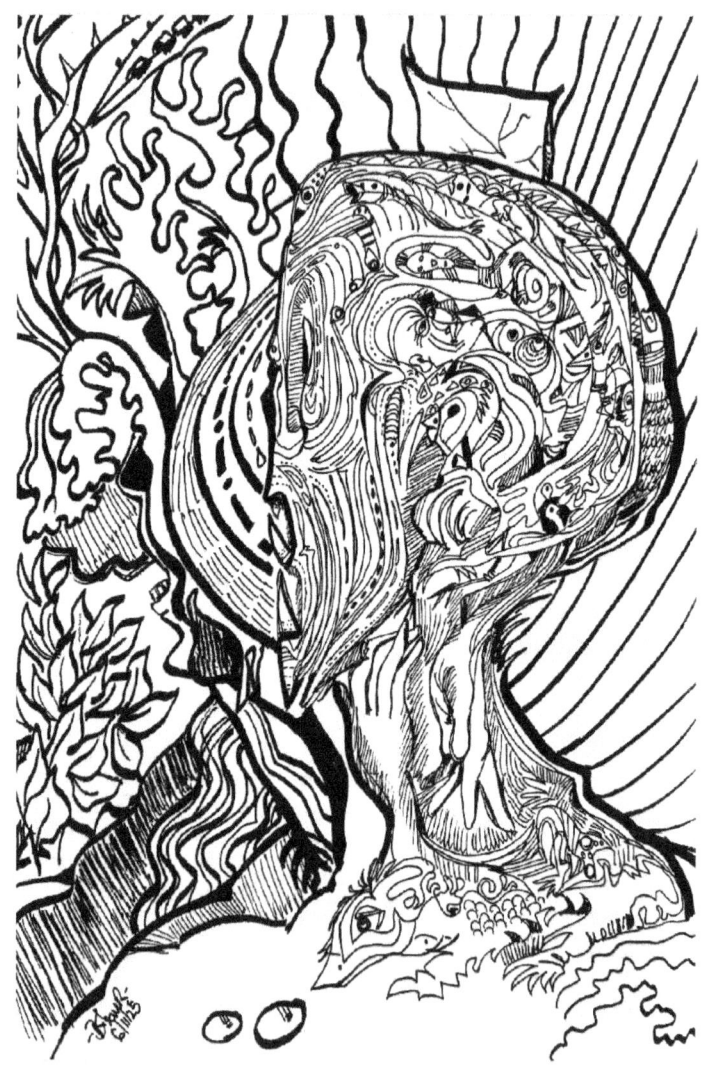

WITHIN A POEM

What's a poem?

Is that what the placid lake

told the lonely poet

Or is it the poet's monologue

with the lake as the audience?

It has elements of both

An ode to life and its woes

with the images of nature

translated into words

born out of febrile passion

or in a fit of utter despair…

The darned fabric of lines

inked with the flowing words

is the balm for the pains

of a perceptible mind…

It would make sense to none

except the restless writer,

who breathes through his words,

the reason for his existence!

The souls of withered blossoms

and the birth pains of the tree

are symbolic of the sensitivity

of the mystery called nature…

The unraveling process of life

is too hard to bear in reality,

the surrealism of a dream

that permeates the verses

is what keeps life afloat…

As the lake meditates

over the melancholy of the day,

receiving the passing rays of the sun

and the morning rains

with equipoise of the mind

like a poem, yet to be written…

FAREWELL TO A WALLABY

A cloudy autumn evening

I pass by a wallaby on the road

it is dead, its head crushed,

savaged by the merciless wheels

of a vehicle on nocturnal prowl;

It had no time to let out a cry

before letting out the soul

into the darkness in the bush,

They say the souls of animals

do not become scary ghosts

unlike the afterlives of humans!

It lay there to be scavenged

not just by the hungry ravens

by also by the van carrying roadkills,

the carcass to be disposed of

without a drop of tear or a prayer,

quite unceremoniously, so to speak…

The walkers follow the trail of life

unheeding the disturbing scene,

Whilst making sure they kept a distance

from the motionless creature…

It would soon be dark

and the clouds would turn into rain,

I hope the body would be buried

unless it becomes food for the foxes,

That is how it works in this world

as they say, the wallaby was just too unlucky!

WORDLESS

In the fleeting smiles

and the barely audible whispers

one seeks permanence

that the world remains static

with the visuals etched on a wall whilst the train is in motion…

One secretively wishes

for the waves of emotions

to be immortalised,

so that he could sail back in time

and revisit those images

like those of an ancient village,

with the characters

that seem all too familiar

despite the strangeness!

That happiness is eternal

the sorrows ephemeral,

and the winds unpredictable

as ordained by destiny

or the key-holder of the mystery,

And that the experience

sweet or sour they maybe

ought to be cherished

in a life of endless possibilities

engraved on waters of transience,

is the lesson from the elders…

That is written on their faces,

smile-less but sentient,

unweathered by the passage of time…

THE UNREAD

There are verses

beyond the conceptual beauty

in the crypts of nature,

The poetry is written

on the lochs and the skies

inked by some unknown,

to be carefully deciphered

by the discerning eyes!

The world of the living

stitched to the running clock

is tumultuous with sounds

and the endless strives

the battles for survival,

masking the letters and lines

and the soulful beauty,

thereby giving an impression

a false one, of life…

The essence is in the silence,

the interludes of placidity,

which, however brief they maybe

wakes one from the dream,

not into the so-called reality

but into a deeper wakeful dream!

The awareness of a synthesis,

an amalgamation of timelines

the intricacies of the genes,

then fills the vagrant mind

creating anxiety and intrigue…

A raindrop of insight

falls from the cosmos,

that space is a mere perception

and that life is a quest

beyond the veneer of sounds,

and that the search is painful

to realise the meaning of nothingness…

THE GHOST

The ghost is in love

with the enchanting moonlight,

and the sweetness of blood

flowing like a river

though the soft thin neck

of the lovelorn woman,

pining over her beloved!

Hiding the malignant eyes

and the sadistic smile

cleverly under the wrinkles

of the undead body

is the vampire of the castle,

the prince of darkness

the lord of the vanquished souls

of long dead women!

Many a crestfallen knight

have lost themselves in the woods

to become menial servants

of the synonym of the devil

cloaked in ancient nobility…

The tall manly figure

that casts no shadow

or his image in the mirror,

with blood on his clawing teeth

and traces of afterlife

within the frame of his fossil

that hasn't perished with time…

In the darkness of antiquity,

through the unlit snowy terrains

unperturbed by the harsh winter

the phantoms of horses gallop,

carrying the erstwhile warlord

crossing the bridges of centuries

to venture deep into the nightmare

birthing within a stormy mind…

THE ENDLESS DREAM

The world is created

not from the tears

of joys and sorrows,

or the fire of aspirations,

But is composed of

the dust of bygone dreams

that are no longer memories…

Forever removed from reality

in the crypts of nature,

abstruse and intriguing

but forgotten and lost

the very next moment

after they reveal themselves,

Though a tangible pain lingers

in a corner of the mind

like a distant serenade

in wintry chill…

The physical world

with its enduring charm is

nothing but a collective dream,

a remembrance of the visions

that constitute the vibrant day

and the stillness of the night

only to be buried,

for the imageries to follow,

the young dreams

born within the minds at rest

the eyes firmly closed,

too early to wake up,

and to callously walk over

the tender souls,

the withered petals of dreams…

A FUTURE TOO BRIGHT

Beautiful jewels of transient joys

skilfully woven into an intransigent fate,

embroidered with silky moonlight

and the gold from the solar mines,

An exquisite work of unmatched art

so delightful for the eyes to behold!

In denial man is, of the impermanence,

holding on to unrealistic hopes

and the highs of an impeccable world

born out of his own imagination…

The stars remind him about death

and the distant constellations

of collective memories of lives once lived…

What's beyond the skin and the flesh?

Is there matter unique to man's life,

something that's distinctly human?

The vision has limiting boundaries

though the restless thoughts travel

through the opened windows of the mind

to assemblies in the universe far away,
where the formless and mysterious shapes
coalesce into cosmic communions;
where stars are reborn within dead shells
and the souls of withered flowers abound…
The man in his abode of glass
in the remote edge of the blue dot
sees nothing but an image of himself
moulded in firmness by sacrosanct beliefs;
To him life revels with flurries of activities
without which he would be a stillborn,
birthed into a day of silent inertness
Dreaded is that meditative experience
where nothing moves, and no company
save an abandoned coffin on the cold floor
holding a dead man, who is his mirror image
…
The illusive dynamism of the day is a mask
that hides the fear that lives within the man,
The fear of death within him, and of lives
that fill the voids unknown to mankind,
Fate! the subaltern of god or god himself?

The tragic twists, the painful interludes

hurt him, forcing him to rethink in loneliness,

and let the sash of his windows slide open

to the "whys" that've eluded even the wise…

Within the drama of fanciful deception

man lives alongside the phantoms,

compelled to ditch his past in forgetfulness

pretending to be innocent and gullible

a fallible lamb lured into the pastures,

green and fertile with promises of the future;

He is naturally in denial about himself,

as a bulwark against nostalgic reversals

into the unsung memoirs of his past,

making him immune to the radiant future

and it's often hailed grail of glories…

SOCIALISATION

The society is a delusion

of a man who is confronted

by the reality of loneliness…

The night that sleeps tight

all alone is the truth;

The day is an apparition

replete with illusive movements!

The satellites eclipse the man

with stringent civil obedience

the least disruptive to status quo

in the ambience of a dream…

Full of life, rich in splendours

most perfect and charming

like an iridescent isle

only to vanish into the night!

Nothing remains,

not even memories

just the man and his self,

a unit of duality

competing with its own shadow…

THE INJURED

I saw a wounded raven

in the worn out backyard

where a half rotten fence stands

reminding me I'm a neighbour

to somebody I don't yet know!

In the freezing weather

the bird limped along

as if hoping to reincarnate

into its past youthful form,

But it was evidently infirm

and quite possibly dying

unbeknownst to itself…

I kept some water in the bowl

on the cold floor of the alfresco

just to lend a helping hand

to a life in crisis;

Little did I expect

to see the raven alive

the following dawn,

when the warm orange of the sun

glazed the frosty grounds…

But to my great surprise

there it was!

Not as a ghost in white

but as the black bird

full of exuberant life at heart

though physically weak and tired,

perched on a mossy parapet

its head turning to and fro

perhaps searching for its flock;

It must be hungry, I thought

every living being is!

I put some breadcrumbs on the floor

and retreated into my space,

By the time I came back

after the meditation,

the parapet was empty

so was the floor!

At a distance, on the hills

the obedient lambs

competed for fresh green food!

The wounded men

too many in number,

their vulnerable hearts heavy

with the burdensome lives,

journeyed aimlessly

through the spiralling corridors,

not seeking food or water

but to slake their thirst for eternity!

STORIES UNTOLD

The night isn't blind

it's the view from behind

of a life in turmoil,

A vision that the day can't spoil

for man is truthful to his soul

in the silence of his cubby hole,

Starless is the sky at night

but the mind is bright with insight,

He knows not what the night would bring

an ethereal cherub or a bird singing!

Reflecting on the day that has passed by

he's unsure whether it was real or a lie,

The people warring with words

have gone to bed to rest their vocal cords!

Afar in the streets infested with insomnia

the night instils a vague sense of fear,

where a shadow is mistaken for a ghost

searching for what it has lost…

The day was the night's dream

saying which the man's face would beam,

Time must be wrong with the calculations

it takes forever to heal the gashes

that life has wrought on the mortal,

He's in bed with a lot of stories to tell

birthed in the barns of darkness,

The sleepy lambs couldn't care less

But he listens to what the night brings along

hoping that the dream would last for long…

FURY

A fit of fury

is the most complete of blindness!

The storms of rage

so violently shut the doors

that not even an iota of light

is allowed into the distressed mind…

The painfully clenched fists

and the agonising groans

mask any traces of insight,

The love at heart sinks deeper

as if drowning into an abyss

unable to voice its presence!

The quiet longing of the past

replaced by a fearful anxiety,

about, what next?

The years of togetherness

in the garden of life are forgotten,

The magical tree with blossoms

stands before the ruins of a castle

in a wildly disturbing dream

contrasting with the eeriness…

The blindness is insensate

and with reason trampled over

by the hoofs of emotions,

the sleeping volcano erupts

wreaking havoc on life…

The dawn wakes up to regrets

and drops of wasted tears

clinging onto the leafy eyes

of a sleepless night…

The random storm creates nothing

but a destructive deluge of anger

which kills off the seedling beds,

to bring forth poisonous weeds,

which, alas, too bears flowers!

THE SACRED LIE

A life lived just to pay the bills

the beauty of life is what it kills!

The child sees roof in the sky

For the "grown up," it's an illusive lie!

Childhood wasn't about showy joys

nor was it heartless empty noise,

The innocence that once was yet to be lost

would swing back to haunt like a ghost,

when he's indulgent in the adulthood farce

not seeing anymore of those twinkling stars!

They say, the dad shoulders the weight

for the child to reach for the lofty height!

The carefree lad playing pranks

was a gullible apostle of ignorance,

that was incredulous, but exciting

making a life one real living "thing!"

But, he who made friends with everyone

hadn't matured a spine of his own!

His happiness was his parents' sweat

something that he would soon forget,

So that pain doesn't set his heart on fire

he learns to forget, and becomes a liar!

Of false morals spurious joys, and vain pride

is the adult, sadly the child's other side…

BEYOND AN AUTOGRAPH

What's in the vault

of a man's life?

A life that has seen it all

the sourness of truths

and the sagging sorrows?

A man who braved all seasons

the winds and the tides,

the highs and the lows

the precipitous drops

from the dreamlike loftiness…

In short, a weather beaten life

well rounded and resilient

so to speak…

What's at the core of his life,

the vibrantly pulsating heart

in the body of his unwritten history?

The fading shreds of memory

some scintillating imageries

a share of sobering afterthoughts

maybe, a hidden love privy to himself,

or a forever secret for the grave

Or is it something else?

Friendship is everlasting, they say

a unique bond that stays on

as an emblazoned memory in the living,

That which is deep and undefinable

and is intertwined with the heart,

one that's beyond genetic brotherhood,

could be at the centre of life…

Knowing that life is ephemeral

and would perish into nothingness,

But to have a good friend by the side

is comforting for the emancipated soul…

Is that not the raison d'être

for a human being on earth,

To be a truly good friend,

to live amongst those transparent minds

and die as a friend?

TEAR DROP ON A MAPLE LEAF

The scarred face of a maple leaf

carries a tear drop,

of a dead and forgotten poet

who once lamented about loss…

The same vagrant mind

which was wildly excited

at the birth of the winter sun,

rolling naked over the grass

to be touched by the raindrops,

floated like a vain log of wood

over the placid waters of melancholy…

He oft wondered about transience

of light and darkness,

The night unfathomably deep

holding the souls of dead stars

had more meaning, than the day

skittering up the hills, to vanish

and die, cloaked in blackness…

Life was about loss, he thought

the end of life was indeed

a gain of the unseen fabled heavens!

The flower blooms aware of death

to be buried in the consciousness

of the many eyed living…

The short tenure doesn't deter

the butterfly from winging its way

to the mystic places of its dreams!

The swiftly perishing night

creates tantalising images whilst asleep

only to turn into dust at dawn…

Everything belongs to a dream,

to the untrammelled imagination

of something unearthly, ethereal,

Or every single thing dreams

in its own singular way,

What's gained within the spectacle

is lost and cremated within it,

Life was nothing but a visual collage

and man tries to find coherence

knowing it is not meant to be so…

Such were the streams of thoughts

of his tempestuous mind,

The tears he shed for the wastage of life

and its endless misery and conflicts,

has condensed into one solitary drop

and still sits on the maple leaf,

which too is sadly dead…

LASTING PEACE

Peace is not the opposite

of the demon, called war!

It is the tranquility

of the inner self

that defines every human being…

It is not a worthless truce

signed by warring factions

mediated by some scavengers,

It flows with spontaneity

through an unscripted path,

filling the vacuum of existence

uplifting the tormented soul…

It has no date of expiry,

even after the last gasp of breath

the peace holds,

translating itself into eternity,

binding itself upon the grieving mass

not as a flimsy veil of solemnity

but as a poignant tearful elegy

a heart rendering musical piece

that accompanies to the grave…

Peaceful is the flower

that meditates over the tomb,

Its vibrance is drifting away

its death is no longer obscure,

a life torn away from the stalk

to befriend the dead man

like the jewellery of a pharaoh

in the cold lonely recess…

Peaceful is the meadow

that is empty at night,

devoid of anxious men and women,

who've no time for a quiet sunset

but pretend to be busy

in their worlds of thoughts!

Peaceful is the sun

rising out of its own accord,

painting gold on the pavement

where a destitute has spent his night…

Peaceful is the moon

that has witnessed many a life

and many a death on a far off earth,

from the gambolling colt

to the ambitiously virulent man,

every living being unaware

that life is but a reunion

with an imaginative future

that is buried amongst dead stars…

THE GHOST AND THE LAMP

A crowd of people

real faces, real chatter

dispels all the ghosts

dispatching *them* to oblivion…

A crowd of thoughts

confusing, conflicting

invites the same ghosts

to plunder the inner peace!

The thought ought to be singular

in its perspective,

rooted not in the peat of antiquity

but in the solid ground of rationality…

One single shining light

does the job of thousands,

piercing the darkness at its core

digging a deep hole in its heart,

thus opening the membranous eyes

of tender foetal brightness,

the harbinger of wisdom…

The ghost falters in brightness

the miasma of despair melts,

shorn of the ubiquity of darkness

paving way not for a fabled angel

but an iota of wisdom,

that like a solitary lamp

in the midst of a night in the desert

would attract many an aspiring soul!

ENCLOSED

Claustrophobia isn't weird!

It's only natural,

Enclosed has been the space

tucked in between the walls

impermeable to vision,

right from his inception…

The ten months of incarceration

were spent in total blindness

but with immense acoustic sharpness!

He could hear his mother

singing a soulful tune

though neither she nor he

knew anything about music,

He could sense her warm breaths

that fed life into his tiny vessels,

And on some cold nights

when it was lonely and quiet,

he could clearly hear her

sobbing wistfully on the pillow

though he didn't know why,

For, he thought he was her happiness,

A joy so real and love so pure

that everything else is forgotten,

But, that wasn't the case it seems

as the mother too was an erring human;

When he was finally born

one morning, after a rainy night

and smelt the mould in the farmhouse,

he was once again confined

to the walled space in a wooden cradle,

an antique parachuted from the attic!

Encased within the walls of an old bedroom

sparingly furnished and looking bleak,

Walled from above by a tiled roof

that leaked the rains and sunlight!

When he opened his naive eyes

and matured fast enough

to grasp the colours around him,

the cloudless blueness in the sky

appeared to be yet another wall!

Walls vertical! Walls horizontal!

Walls not just physical

But of tribe, faith, hierarchy,

the endless schisms of "isms,"

Love so untrue and hatred so visceral

and walls becoming so rigid with time,

that he has no memory of freedom,

All that remains is the closeness

of the empty space,

and the dread that the sky is closing down

like an iron lid over a glass bottle

with the fly trapped within it

haplessly flipping its wings…

TOO GOOD TO BE REAL!

"It isn't a fake!"

I have been advised

to remind myself, again!

Like a killer's smile

the smile ought to be real

trustworthy, not malignant!

I see this "painting" on the wall

interred within a golden shell,

Why do I keep fidgeting

on the realisation it is "digital?"

The piece has human elements

an effort, a genuine one too,

but it hasn't got the fingerprints

of an artist who felt the pain,

like that of a mother in labour

lovingly birthing her child…

Yet it isn't a fake,

it is the future, they say,

of what has been called art;

It isn't man vs machine anymore

but a collaborative teamwork,

The idea is appealing

the produce alluringly colourful,

But it hasn't got something

that plants it in the heart,

something that's uniquely human

the vision of one pair of eyes

the pain of one heart

to create not a spectacle

but a deeply personal document

that is reclusive and distant,

Yet it feels intimate

a testament of humanity,

detached from the digital deluge…

A PLENTIFUL DAY!

The day of happenings

must have been yesterday,

The morning it did rain

the sun was in a pensive mood,

The light had a child's fingers

drawing vague mysterious forms

on the sleepy verdant meadows,

And, as it happens

the night's dreams left no trace

of their being on earth,

leaving the solitude to the man…

Thus the happenings continued

through the day unaffected,

the faltering light of the afternoon

played with the children in the street

the ravens as fervent as ever

debated over a crumb of bread,

The leaves rustled in the mangrove

as a breeze visited the canopy,

The city's canal stalled with its infinite filth

pretended to flow unhindered!

The mosquitoes harmonised with the rats

as the masters of their own microcosms;

The street lamps were meditative

prayerful to be enlightened at dusk,

The skies rejoiced at the end

of a day on the remote earth,

draped in their arresting robes,

with a shade of deep crimson

where the mounts bonded with the seas…

The stars formed giant constellations

in cosmic geometric patterns,

The bands of nameless nocturnals

emerged from their hiding holes

preying on the singing insects,

The woods reverberated with the chorus

of crickets and unknown souls,

The resurrection of the soul of the day

happened at the anointed hour

in the recesses of a long night,

As the pulpit in heavens readied itself

to welcome the birth of a dawn,

the narrow alleyways dimly slept

housing all the homeless unfortunates on earth…

GRIEF

Grief

has a state of permanence

that nothing in mortal mind

can erase or make fainter,

The pain is knifed into deep

into the mysterious cells

of the grieving heart

that holds the cup of love,

It is not a superfluous tattoo

but an indelible birthmark

that accompanies the vagrant soul

through the pains of rebirths…

Loss is the essence of existence

The memories of the floral bough

under which the siblings once played,

the castles built of the golden sands

in the distant dreamy seashores,

the touch of the pink hands

and the hidden tears in the eyes,

they resurge with a renewed frenzy

devoid of the grainy haziness of lost times

creating a profound sense of loss,

that bites at the core of the heart

not with a blunt savage force

but as a sharp permeating sting

from some unknown cosmic insect,

that rattles the calamitous mind

in the waves borne within a storm…

The bereaved one is washed ashore

to the dreamy playground of siblings,

and after a listless wandering

searching for something from the past,

He realises that their tiny castle of yore

eaten up by time, is there no more…

LI"F"E

What could one call

this evanescence called life?

A lie, a misnomer

or a bitter truth,

of being entirely perishable…

The insufferable terminal agony

the inevitable end,

to be draped in white sadness

scented with profuse tears…

Or the beginning

of an uncharted journey

into the womb in another space?

To become a nonhuman

who has unlearned his life,

A wiped and clean slate

ready for the cosmic alphabets…

To become a non-substance

weightless than the tiniest of atoms

unyoked from the dial of time…

To be the soul of a leaf

that prided at the vantage point

nurtured by the giant Palmyra,

to become the shade for a lost ant

and to be buried by the passing rains…

The myopic eyes are not deceptive

the vision but can only stretch that far,

to the solitary grave beneath the tree

covered by unheeded wild flowers…

The beholder of all the sweet lies,

the man drenched in the visual deluge

would still pass by that graveyard,

cautious and speeding his steps,

anxious about freed up ghosts!

The mirage of the day would end

and it would be starless windy night,

The darkness that he's naturally fearful of,

the reminder of the invisible avenue

leading to the mossy paths of the galaxies…

THE ANNIVERSARY OF A DREAM

It was lighter than the wind

more invisible, more impalpable

but delicately perceivable...

They call it an illusion

I would call it a dream,

a bright mysterious space

in which I lost count of time,

As a weightless image

which could think like a human

I permeated the buildings

made of ageless sandstones,

where I met those familiar faces

still alive in the atmosphere

of childhood unspoilt by time!

I became part of the drama

knowing it must have an end

but weightless that I was

I henceforth moved hither tither

with such amazing rapidity

like an unhinged astronaut!

I met a family of patients

who've apparently been entrapped

in some cryptic cult of insanity!

They were scary like apparitions

within a mauve stone mansion

which spoke of a wealthy past;

I procrastinated thinking it was prudent

to avoid taking the risk,

But when I finally met them

having been dropped off in my car,

to my surprise there were humans too!

The old lady had an infection

and I felt obliged to treat her,

I was wrongly prejudiced, I told myself

it was contrary to medical ethics,

a lesson has been learnt

perhaps for the future…

Last night I flew into my friend's house

the immediate neighbour in my past,

like a broken kite in the sky of freedom!

The rooms from my childhood visions

kept me spirited as the adult

who was seeking earnestly

about something he was unsure of!

The images move at a rhythmic pace

cohesively delivering a unique experience

that moves me from within,

transforming me from a man of reality

sinking in the rising seas of existence

to an obligate dreamer who stays afloat!

In my dreams, I feel like a feather

that ought to be beautiful to behold,

But a feather is a fallen piece of mirage

broken off and orphaned by the body…

The window blinds can't be parted,

the memory has faint glimpses

like a bird that defied the rules of death,

the sole survivor from the festive season

of a bygone era…

Weightless though I am

within the intricate matrix of dreams,

the loftiness is a meditative experience

defying the solidness of logic

in the fortress of reality

that a human being is bound to live!

I become part of the floral wind

or a constituent in the assembly of raindrops,

I once again become the foetus

that didn't get sleep enough

within the womb of short gestation

of his mother who birthed him

out of desperation to see his rosy face!

On the anniversary of his final dream

within that dark cozy space,

as the stars that had long been dead

cast their shadows in the rain clouds

he desires to be unborn,

to break the bonds of the living

and be the grainy image in a dream,

just so that he could love his life again…

THE ANNIVERSARY OF THE SOUL

A day approaches

with its feet uncertain

whether to knock the door!

The room that harbours

one traumatic year of pain

and a lifetime of memories…

The chairs had been occupied

by the days begone,

The old clock turns a circle

announcing in solemn silence

that it has been an year,

a whole year!

that four seasons have passed

since the absence of a life,

its exile from the planet…

The curtains flail in the wind

as the monsoon hovers around,

The room is visibly empty

the chairs free to occupy,

Light glimmers and fails

like the gasps of the living,

The day takes its seat

struggling to contain the disquiet

just to register its presence,

The walls are plain and gloomy,

Not a single picture exists

of the uniquely beautiful soul,

The images of life splintered

and suffused with dreamy visuals,

within a timeless ethereal space…

The clock obliges nature

the needles traversing the dial

and it would become another circle,

another year, and yet another…

The day would vacate its seat

rightfully, at the midnight hour

after a deeply silent meditation,

like the soul in cosmic solitude…

The anniversary comes to a pause

the fragrant candle melts into wax

glued on to the hearts of the living

as a memory, of a day,

an dreamy pictorial monument

of human endurance of pain…

JOURNEYING AT NIGHT

The seat by the window

is a special one!

It's closer to the night

close to the drifting clouds

and the reluctant rain drops

creeping along their own rail tracks!

It is closer to sleep

for, darkness induces sedation,

in tune with the diurnal rhythm!

It is closer to the music,

the background score of darkness,

one that's unheard in daylight

but abounds the night!

It is closer to the homes

beside the winding rail tracks,

where children asleep in their beds

draped in thick warm blankets

dream of fantastic train journeys

through the flowery forests

in the distant moonlit skies!

It is closer to myself,

the passenger on an uncertain earth,

journeying towards the unknown…

The seat is special

so is life!

THE SHADOW ON THE GLASS

Nothing like a pot of tea

poured into a docile glass,

to importune the reluctant skies

not to delay the inevitable,

the downpour any longer!

The day has been overcast

the humidity too intense

the tumult insufferably long

to the urban hearts!

The heat is formidable, it spices up

the petulant emotions,

the countless pollens from trees

conspire with the mounts of dust

as sweat pores fume with rage!

Yet the mind seeks respite

in the den in the city corner

where broken men are cloistered

to share the travails of their journeys

through their translucent eyes,

as the rustic samovar wheezes

to create the concoction

that would soothe the ache

of the vagrant travellers…

The shop has the old cuckoo clock

a sculpted wooden marvel

but with an empty dial,

The bird doesn't sing that often

But when it does

it rains joy in the lonely hearts

pining over their lost loves

buried in the marshland of monsoons,

The bird has been dead for long

but the music isn't…

The liquid filled with unsung lives

is fast steaming into vapour

the invisible bonding with the skies,

that remain as reticent as ever…

The half empty teapot

under the longstanding umbrella

is the silent prelude to the night;

As the crowd disintegrates
in despair, casting sly glances
at the thickly veiled opaque skies,
a thunder gently rumbles
and then all is quiet!
It is reminiscent of the school bell
dispersing the weary children,
to trundle across to their homes
after a long day!
The tea-seller would soon vanish
into some mysterious space in darkness,
hoping to reemerge with dawn
with his tray of freshly baked bread
and a rekindled samovar
to churn out copious pots of tea!
The men have already forgotten
the little chats that they had,
They believe that they ought to,
as it is deemed to be a hindrance
to the harsh reality of their journey
that could deviate them
from the slithery paths they pursue…

From the charpoy on the tiled terrace

overlooking the ancient quarters

of the city of shadows,

the man has an epiphany!

That the moon is a giant saucer

a cool plate of exquisite beauty

exuberant with milk

bursting to pour out with elegance

to slake the endless thirst

of the gawking earth!

A RAIN IN THE DESERT

If it doesn't rain in the city

it's too humid,

The stuffy sweltering heat

is insufferable…

If one doesn't hear

any whisper of conversations

the overwhelming silence

is truly suffocating…

If there's no ventilation

in the cluttered room of thoughts,

No window to invite the light

it is too dark and depressing…

If the clouds are indecisive

and the rains play hide and seek,

the city is one big chimney

emitting toxic fumes…

If there's no pot of tea

the epicentre of evening chatters,

If the samovar goes cold

the evening is stale and barren…

If there is no rain of sensory inputs

pouring through the ceiling,

the thoughts are limbless apparitions

buried in the four walled grave…

The earth has vacant seizures

in the quietness of estrangement,

when tongues are obliged

to be the garb of muteness…

The moonless nights are pensive

about the blankness of the canvas,

If only the humans could speak

surmounting their paralysed vocal cords!

If there was no peace in solitude

and if it was as thorny as hell,

Man wouldn't have survived

when cast away to some earthly isle…

If the body doesn't decay

the memories still would, sometime;

Death has made man a spiritual being

for the preservation of his self…

If only the eyes could weep

shunning the shroud of adulthood,

it would have rained at heart

to fill the wells of acceptance of grief…

Sleep evades the lachrymose eyes

shadowing the wandering mind,

Dreams abound in the isle of insomnia

to tackle the pernicious melancholy…

If only the winds would blow

teasing out the tears from the clouds!

The fluttering thoughts awaken the heart

Hoping that the stillness doesn't last for long…

The world is a patchily green desert

where humans have come to graze,

The oasis is nothing but his dream

a fantasy, mirroring his uncertain life…

When the meadow is dead

at the peak of the unforgiving heat,

It may rain, he still believes earnestly

as he is devoted to his dreams…

The pilgrims who have passed this way

sought the wisdom of the earth,

In lone rooms of ancient Nalanda

Did they find heaven in the parchments?

If one of those scholars could live on

for centuries together, without death,

Man would've known the pain of the search

to rationalise his earthly existence…

But the ancients have died

passing the genetic batons on to posterity,

Does the library scroll have a bloodline

that interconnects the generations of wisdom?

Happiness is a superlative feeling,

sadness makes one more grounded,

The tallest branches are worldly and fickle

the stronger roots seek other dimensions…

If there is no temptation

what's the need for a moral dictum?

The nature is attractive, painful is the lure

that pulls one towards it, knowing there is no fruition…

Is wisdom the tree or the fruit,

Wherefrom is the seed of fertile thoughts?

The winds are invisible, like gods

The ghosts of men appear in the dreams though…

It hardly rains inside the room

though it is a deluge in the yard,

the roof is strong, the windows fastened

the light aches to enter the dormitory in slumber…

In between the stations of life and death

the populace transits through the hall,

where broken timelines are infused

with the magic of dreams infesting the travellers…

How common is a shared dream

on the deserted table of two travellers?

The umbilical cord dissipates the strangeness

they're not one, but two, entwined in a singular dream…

They've known each other at the diner,

where the met as two wayfarers,

But with one eye contact, their tracks fused

into one journey, in a remote life in antiquity…

The residue of a morning shower lingers

on the window panes and the corridor,

The smell of fresh earth is in the air

a fragrance of new life, made of clay and fire…

If only one could passionately love

oblivious to the fissiparous world,

Love that unconditionally permeates everything

that even a saint would struggle to achieve…

The caterpillar journeys along the half dead leaf

as the mourners gather around the coffin,

The life is frivolous but endures

in some form, though death happens in between…

Humanity is the height of insanity
increasingly endowed with intellect
but incredulous about love
and the universality of his own condition!

This is a park where two lovers meet
hugging and exchanging vain kisses,
only to part in tears, breaking their promises,
The trees are wise, for they've seen it all…

The showers have commenced
only to fizzle away after the outburst,
The lamps glimmer to wipe away the darkness
from the street, as half drenched strangers pass by…

Under the nameless tree, circle the flies,
the damsels of the monsoon night,
They seek the essential pleasures of life
the lizard lies in waiting, behind the cornice…
The foragers speak in their mother tongues
indecipherable to the naive human,
The flies denote the cycle of life
from the mouthful of food to an inevitable death…

The world is replete with scavengers

life is something else's food,

The tenacious web is extensive

spanning the entirety of the universe…

The spider is the master of trickery,

astute and silent, in waiting,

The preys are noisy and vibrant

unaware of their fateful nocturnal journey…

In between the monosyllables

there is a pause, a prologue,

an anticipation that there's more to life

than what's apparent to the naked eyes…

The dog senses danger,

Apprehensive of possible extinction,

Is he fearful about death

a mortal fear that the trembling human experiences?

The darkness is the cradle of ghosts

pale white formless creatures without life,

They may have lived or not lived at all

The mind is a porous basket, through which they escape!

The night dictates the preamble to freedom

the loner is captivated by its silence,

Amidst the humdrums and the vicissitudes

a wave of music exists in the fibre of the night…

How to preclude oneself from life

to skip the rotations in the spinning wheel,

Who would want to be that guinea pig

a fluffy toy in the hands of the unseen?

It isn't fair, this is a lie,

a charade of vain characters, one dare say

But who's to be blamed for the mishap

The biological conundrum of existence?

The torrid currents are essential

so that one is consciously afloat,

lest he be drowned in his own dream

his fossil never to be recovered again!

The lights keep the promenade aglow

weightless men drift as shadows

Unable to tackle the high winds, the boat

is moored at the union of the sky and the sea…

If the seas aren't calamitous

the captain risks going to sleep,

Zeus loves to be the god of action!

Stay awake! Be alert! The waves rise in an uproar…

The moon fades at the birth of the day,

one light transforms into another,

The world survives as long as there's light

to be resurrected from eternal darkness…

The lyrical flower rests on the lustrous dark hair

the moon lights up the nocturnal nest,

The light scripts primal alphabets of life

on the forest path winding around the rivulet…

Wherefrom does man draw the inspiration

to travel along the lesser known path?

The lost sailors at sea pray for an exit

to evade the trap of the goddess…

Why waste one's thoughts over the seer,

the one who knows the path to wisdom?

He remains elusive, let him be!

It will soon be dawn, be the butterfly seeking daylight…

Tumultuous is life, its intricacies confusing

the despondency grows into depression…

Laughter averts mental disaster, it is precious like water,

There would be wars fought to recapture the ability to laugh!

There is a lot to laugh about, than to weep,

the broken promises would be a good start!

The tearless flies dance around the coffin

unmoved by the engulfing sadness…

On whose domain is man, has he any right to be here,

This land isn't his, nor are the seas,

He belongs to the stars that have long been dead,

he is the epitaph on the tomb of dead stars…

The shadows of lightning in the heavens,

are they reflections of the extinct gods?

Who knows where they restfully sleep?

Probably within the catacombs of ancient minds…

The mutations keep happening, humans change

their outlooks get transformed irrevocably,

The fly on the pendulum is oscillating

bringing forth changes to its moral properties…

The dissected body is rejoicing

at the discovery of wisdom within it,

The students in white coats are ghosts

loitering in the treeless graveyard…

He who spent hours talking to the body

failed the objective examination,

he shouldn't have been conversing

believing the cadaver had a soul!

It was wrong that he had a feeling

for the body that had long been dead,

bathed in chemicals to be dissected,

The dead log of wood no longer feels…

They create horror stories out of the dead,

thrilling those fearful of their own deaths,

Men are nothing but walking ghosts

shadowed by the callous grim reaper…

The banister disappears all of a sudden

revealing the depths of the stairwell,

How unconscious man is while he is alive

about the illusiveness of his realities!

The romantics adored consumption

to be deceived and devoured by death,

Yet they created phenomenal works of art

depicting the surreal beauty of life!

What if this is all an extended farce

the dead ancient gods playing jokes!

Man mirrors the plight of his forebears

acutely conscious of his predicament…

It is a shabby morning, the skies overcast,

the vehicles briskly move like phantoms,

hooting and howling, creating a ruckus,

the circus of life is in full swing!

To the school, some to the hospital
others elsewhere, the paths diverge,
The man at home is at crossroads
procrastinating over which way to go!

He has carried the same school bag
trodden along the same path of pupils,
dreaming of the eternal sunshine
embroidering the oft beaten paths…

The excitement is wild for the child
borne out of nothing in particular,
For, every single day is unique and special
designed for the young man to explore!

Was that a reverie of the shepherd
who loved to dream at the hillside?
How empty and meaningless his world would be
if or when he wakes up to the reality!

The gossamer of dreams is enticing

the spider waits patients with the bait,

ready to entrance the wanderer's mind

the drama plays on stage for its own pleasure!

The future is candid but won't be lucid,

the violence is written on the wall

Blood begets blood, peace remains a hope

a flower that blooms only in dreams…

Beyond the perception of the senses

there must be a world of some sort, man thinks,

that is resplendent with *real* flowers

Ironical it is, that reality exists within a fantasy!

Man is a chromophobe, fearful of colours,

but he believes in them as they're are illusions,

The dream has no colours on its palette

The easel doesn't know what's being painted…

There is brightness in those eyes

that sit in the sockets of youthfulness,

the unabashed honesty of the light

there's a sun in every candlelight…

The clouds have transient colours

the illusion creates a sense of permanence

Nothing changes, except the perception

the ants float on the waters with solid faith…

The war is the exteriorisation of the turmoil

of the beleaguered minds,

The serpent stockpiles its venom for seeking food

Man knows not what to do with his poison!

One looks for interpretations

the metaphors hidden in the imageries,

Does the skylark think the same as man,

as it breezes towards the illusive skies?

Every moment is an unseen funeral,

the eulogies are read in absolute silence,

Man fears being buried with passing time

he groans in agony, from the tombs of forgetfulness…

The man wonders how the skies appeared to him

when he was a child, was it vast or a miniature?

He's unsure, but it was certainly more beautiful

As he often felt he belonged there…

After a lull, sleep arrives, followed by a dream

The long corridor has ghosts, with friendly expressions!

Thinking from within the dream, he has a premonition

that he has seen it all, the storyline is familiar…

What if this is a replay of some unknown past,

played out as life and dreams in equal proportions?

The veneer of illusion is dense, it can't be lifted

even by the most irradiant of sun rays…

The mystery deepens, as man loves the intrigue

the path bifurcates into an alter life,

full of metaphorical allusions through a collage

The fawn crosses the leafy path, stares at him and vanishes!

The rains are about to gatecrash into the dawn,

the clouds have been patient all night,

But it has rained torrentially throughout the dream

of one man, which he alone has perceived…

He aspires to be lofty, detached from the ground

to have an aerial view of the coffin,

the cache of memories covered with dead flowers

for he doesn't want to be one amongst them…

Does he wish for a prenatal clairvoyance

even before the foetal dream is born in his mind?

The imagery, he thinks, is his bygones

in the abandoned shell in a pristine seashore…

The meteors shoot across the dark skies

searching for the vestiges of the umbilical cord,

blood spills into the intransigent clouds,

the moon wades into a dreamy thinness…

Why am I here? asks the man

reflecting the same pangs of his ancestors,

The gametes are alive in the genes

the dreams of the caveman survives through posterity…

His mind is unsettled with doubts,

shadows veil the ghosts, predators abound in darkness,

gods are forever asleep, oblivious to the happenings

The impermanence is disturbing, the mind rebels…

The heavens must be studded with tombstones

the epitaphs unread by gods and angels,

Only the demons with the man would care

but of what help would that be?

The poet births the moon every night

It gives him a purpose, a reason;

The labouring is painful, but there is a beauty in it

Should a poet ever be drawn into such an illusion?

The wavelets are lullabied by the seas

nestling in the arms of the moonlight,

The shore is vacant, the murmurs are faint

The rower has lost sight of the future, the night is too dark…

The glow worms are time capsules

that hold the sap of dreams,

They create phantasms within the cave

within which moments of life stay afloat…

"We once had a common ancestor!"

who said that first, the fish or the bird

The amphibian takes flight with its wings

colluding with the fanciful man in the skies…

How to combat the absurdity of reality,

other than meek acceptance or a life in denial?

The ripples in the river of imagination are relentless,

Man can survive only through living within his dreams…

Let not the paint dry

let it be a rivulet running down the plain wall

The stubbornness of reality shouldn't deter the man

to disentangle the strands of the web he has found himself in!

The father is the school, a singular teacher

the custodian of the child, the flower bud

He is the wisdom that should be imbibed

to shield the bloom from the dangers of naivety…

He inhabits those mountain peaks

where no son can aspire to reach,

The son is a horse riding through the dreams

saddled with the inheritance of memories…

If only the winglets of the butterfly were his,

to be birthed seamlessly from the womb of life,

He seeks the realms of eternity

Every son believes in that dream, where his father awaits him…

If only the tumults were impermanent,

if only the cacophony would subside into silence!

The cashmere shawl that covers the dreaming man

is comforting but it too is illusive…

I'm the tree and the fruit, thinks the forlorn man

both appetisers for the palate of time,

The great sages have died, their bodies decayed

Unstoppable is the giant wheel of destiny…

He refills his pen with the ink of philosophy

to jot down his anxieties to the fullest expression,

The parchment bears the pain imparted by the mind

the goat knows not its skin would one day be etched with human wisdom!

The wanderers in the hills meet

only in the hallways in their dreams,

They pass by unseen to each other's eyes

for they are yet to attain the chalice of immortality…

Men are unable to bear the heat of the truth

they disintegrate themselves into pools of tears

Scalded, wounded and scarred are the mortals

sacrificing their conscience for the pettiness of comfort…

If one hasn't touched the wild flower

he hasn't had the good fortune of living,

If he even hasn't ever seen one

he's yet to be born!

The fairies evade the dreams

reticent to fly into the surreal terrains,

Man is an angel expelled from the darkness

his wings planted on the shoulders of his mind…

The confluence of the sun and the seas

that's where life ends and death begins, he thinks,

The line that divides the two becomes flat

reflecting the stillness of the heart...

Man is reborn after the expiry of his childhood

he toddles along the convoluted tracks

where the nicely smiling grownups play villainy

weaponising their petty egos...

The tree leans towards the roof in the storm

seeking rescue from the onslaught of age

The arborist is precise, the axe is apathetic

killing and reducing the tree to wood, for the fire...

The physician knows the ins and outs of the disease

his wisdom impeccable, his methods meticulous,

He can see the gate of which he is the keeper

which once opened, life is locked out forever...

The ward has blue walls, the beds are white

the faces of occupants pale, their frames gaunt

Angels of life whiz around with the sour concoctions

that would rescue the sufferers from the reaper of death…

Behind the closed door of the washroom

One can faintly hear the suppressed cries

of someone who has lost his dear one,

The unwritten epitaphs are the most poignant…

The doctor positions himself behind the film

that segregates him from his patient,

The anxiety of death within the human is infective

the physician feels the sting, but pretends to be brave…

The rounds are over, it is coffee time

to gossip about the trivia of the *normal* world

That is deliberate, to amputate oneself from the pain

the pernicious misery, the endless saga of human suffering…

Man stares at the ceiling, examining the cobwebs
while the physician examines his rickety chest;
Their minds are travelling in parallel tracks,
the patient is piquant at the travesty of natural justice…

The hospital is misery personified
lives reduced to mere bodies in tiny spaces,
to be prodded and studied with clinical acumen
Ironical it is, that life rejuvenates within those tombs!

Men undertake pilgrimage to the holy shrines
seeking repentance for their litany of misdoings,
The hospital is where gods go on pilgrimage
to self-realise the irrelevance of their mythical legacy…

The electric currents acutely pierce the precordium
giving a jolt to the mad run of the heart,
the gears shift and life resumes in normal rhythm,
The body is an evolved machine prone to errors
it ought to be corrected by another machine!

The salt levels drop, the mercury column falls

cold sweats appear on the forehead, the heart flutters,

Humans swing into action to rescue the fallen

Time is precious, every second lost the shadow death advances…

Whose cart is the bull pulling along

petrified of the merciless lashes,

Is man the driver or the poor animal

burdened with the sorrows and miseries?

The land is unfamiliar, the paths obscured

by the fog of tangled memories

Which way should it go? the animal doesn't think

The man with the whip does, or does he?

The interludes have been silent, barring the bells

jingling from the neck of the animal,

The prescient birds have paused their warbling

The veil of the futuristic time capsule is lifted without human awareness…

The light recedes, there's the house amidst the weeds
with a lone fire alight at the hearth;
On the mantle there rests peacefully a stiletto
aching to pierce the wandering heart…

The tombs of yesterdays are buried in darkness
moments levitate into the moist air
encapsulating the forgotten memories,
time is sharp, the dagger has tinges of warm blood…

The flame from the earthen oil lamp
throws a patch of light on the mouldy wall,
Curious figurines in ochre shed their invisibility
Ghosts survive within the dilapidated minds…

What brings one to a house with no doors,
where mysteries dance to an ancient rhythm?
The man stands on the wooden floor transfixed,
the animal is unaffected, under the moonless sky…

The man forges a bond with the abandonment,

the house is not a shelter, it is a tomb

an impersonal force has drawn him to the woods

to see the light, the frivolous flickering light…

In the deepest depths of solitude

man does not hope to gain any company,

The nature has withdrawn into a shell

the air stands still with the lack of motivation…

Many a time he has read his own obituary

knowing not which one of those is true,

the words are camouflaged with plenitude of tears,

empty expressions that come not from the heart…

The one who lived there had died ages ago

shrivelling into a bony mass that moths wouldn't touch

Man walks into the hollow that hides the fossil

acutely aware that the skeleton resembles his own!

Man is all bones, like the deer or the elephant
the skin dies, the flesh decays, the embers remain as the skeleton,
The evidence of his life, the residue of his phantasms
the forensic truth, the finality of a finite span…

There is no poetry etched on those ribs
that once caged the love for the dear ones,
No portrait exists of a soul, the eternal fragment of life…
The frescos in the skies dissolve into colours
the figures steeped in mystery weave cloudy robes…

He can see a fawn on the primitive land
that stretches between the two walls,
It is limp and hopping, searching for its mother
The childlike eyes blinded with fear of some unknown predator!

It could be him, reminiscent of his past life
a child desperate to be back in the arms of his mother,
The anxiety is mounting, foolish is the caprice
that has drawn him into the gawking wilderness…

The disparaged insect wakes up in a tousle

unsure about the flimsy margins of reality,

The lamp burns, it is irresistibly attractive

how could a flicker of hope be so exuberant!

The walls speak of chambers beneath them,

the vertical fall has commenced already!

The insect has its world tilted like a ball

Could it be an inferno underneath the logs of time?

Thoughts fuelled by the demons of fear

penetrate the fissures in the ancient floors,

The eye pressed hard against the creaking wood

can only see fathomless darkness, like never before…

The strained ears sense the vague painful cry of an animal,

like that of a bull, entrapped in the underworld!

How did it get there, from being the cart puller

to an organism, a meek sacrificial animal?

Is this the abattoir of time, where lives pass through

stripped bare to the bone, the carcass scavenged upon

by the remorseless apathetic insects?

Where's the room for penitence, the ostiary to open the door

…to heaven?…

The light that casts no trace of a shadow!

that's a frightening thought in a lively mirror,

The pernicious loneliness is petrifying

The dead animal must be turning into cubes in a broth…

The circles in the well, the strata of hell

how deep are they? maybe as deep as death?

What instils life into the countless demons?

to guard and torture the captured souls?

Man yearns for the faintest string of music

his heart roiled by the surmounting fears,

Panic recedes into the catacombs of inertia

the psyche alone survives the calamity of the soul…

Torn apart between the two worlds,

parallel ones that have nothing visible in common

The anxious real and the sublime surreal

Which one should man believe in?

In which world do the unseen gods dwell?

They're intertwined with the calm subconscious

and the febrile palpitating conscious!

The lines segregating the two have vanished abruptly!

A dying body can never be absolutely happy

Man's rat racing on his toes is because of his woes!

Either he treats death as a foregone conclusion

or simply pretend the coffin life doesn't exist!

He doesn't see or hear the beauty of music

but he is drawn towards the eulogy

the chorus of obituaries over the dead,

Beyond the doors of solemnity is his afterlife!

Man is a bird with his wings in disuse
atrophied and never able to fly!
He aspired for the skies, but is wasted on land
bowed in the winds of his existential struggles!

Why is there no uniformity amongst men?
The peculiar creatures with capacious craniums
their thoughts differ, the anxiety is the same
as that of the bull yoked to the wheel of death…

Who stole the man from his paradise of peace?
Why is he on the fringes, facing the amorphous demons?
The questions form anxious nebulae within the clouds,
The plains are distant, away from human reach…

He steps over a thorn from the primitive cactus,
the blood streams and stains the floor,
It creates a luminescence, a crimson world
faces appear on the wall, with dysmorphic features…

He has known them before

or are they ghosts untwined from the future?

Love is lost, to be resurrected with hope

Time keeps vigil as the grave keeper…

The stain of umbilical blood is permanent

that ghosts have the natal dent on their bellies,

the prisoners of some god's fantastic dream,

the unfortunate outcast of the antique heavens…

The flower is seated within the painting

that emerges from the angry red wall,

It is lively but dead, but for how long?

the painter feels the urge to ask, but the walls have deaf ears!

The petals are the wings of forgotten angels

harmonising into a tableau of vision,

It is a poetic piece that has no words

the music is in the silence that abounds…

Is there any room for reason within a dream,

as man strives to disentangle himself from

the happenings?

Only to wade deeper into the marshlands of passing imageries

He is entrapped in the gorge that nosedives into a deep valley…

The house will collapse, the woods will

implode

the forest burning, the nests empty…

The dust of the dream would escape into cosmic space

Never to return to the valleys of the earth again…

One last egg orphaned by its mother

would grace the earth with its lonely presence,

the vestige of a dream, a substance within the amorphous,

What would it contain, the seed of a tempest?

The sun has a giant yellow dial

that has something to do with time,

The star doesn't know where it belongs to

like the man beseeching the eternity,

for the paradise of his mother's womb…

Thoughts are clogged within the vagrant mind

the veins are tremulous with the gush of ancestral blood

The mount disintegrates into another phantom,

Identity dissolves into a sea of nothingness…

The exhausted mother's hand sleeps over her baby

the smothering makes it a blue flower,

Accidental and abrupt is the change in nature

The child is reborn, into a flaccid stillness…

Whose imagination is the realm of silence?

A god's or a man's,

or is it the progenitor of all imaginations?

The wooden floor squeals, breaking the harmony…

The man at the tumultuous seas

with waves of wooden splinters!

The floor has sunken into an abyss,

the netherworld that roars from beneath the feet!

The screams are barricaded by the ribs

within which the heart runs like an unbridled stallion,

The novelty of the end is short lived

though it is a ride to the gates of eternity…

BEFORE THE END…

And

at the end

of the thousand year war,

They waited with thumping hearts

and heavily perspiring heads,

A large perfumed cotton towel

gently warmed with ancient oils

and decked with asphodel flowers

of the Elysium of yore

draped their quivering hands…

They had seen enough bloodshed,

heard more than enough ballads

that raved over the myths of the brave!

Vultures with strangely ascetic eyes

had throned themselves over the busts

of the famed conquerors,

Their giant marble marvels

erected over the unmarked graves

of the countless nameless,

the vanquished…

From the blood spilled at Carthage

to the most modern in the line of sacrifice,

From the rage of the almighty Zeus

to the most anonymous of the many gods,

the angry crimson deepened

the pervasive sinister sense

in the otherwise empty skies…

Birds transformed themselves into rats

so that they could avoid the scary skies,

and burrow to be buried alive underground;

The men convened over the mount

awaiting something, an incarnation

that would deliver them from the world

of visceral hatred and unhappiness;

They belonged to all castes and creeds

the wounded, the half slain and the victors

congregating like faithful pilgrims,

but with an unusual demeanour

like that of the midwives

expecting a miraculous delivery!

They barely spoke a word to each other

as they were strangers united

by the havocs of war,

Still ambivalent about violence

and half entrenched in their ideologies,

They had come to believe

that peace is begotten through war

and *only* through war,

That humans are civilised animals

baying for each other's blood

at the opportune moment!

That the violence is in the genes,

the essence of belonging to the species,

the gory script of which is indelible,

and that *only* a state of perpetual war

with all its mushroom clouds of misery

would ensure everlasting peace…

They couldn't stand each other's eyes

fearful of betraying their inner thoughts,

It is true that they hated each other

as much as they despaired over their plight,

Hence with bated breaths

and palpitating hearts

They held up the cloth in their hands

as if it was a gesture of unity

though it was a communion of hatred,

They were expecting the arrival

of peace, the antonym of war!

But for peace to be born

there ought to be the labour of love

through a gestation of understanding…

They craved for the birth of peace

not out of love for each other

but as they were exasperated

by their own misdoings!

The thousand years of constant warring

had reversed their hard earned civilisations

with the inhabitants in cerebral regression;

But the hate infiltrating their marrows

had concealed the reality of their decline,

Darkness ruled over the world

and the barren minds of its occupants…

The red clouded face of the heavens

brought forth no peace,

not even a drop of joyful tear!

Over the slowly disintegrating mountain

they stood like vain lifeless statues

to descend to the blood soaked plains

to resume the relentless fighting

and die as bipedal worms…

A LULLABY

My child!

The skies will no longer be blue

cloudless and heavenly

the exuberant face of paradise…

It will be deep crimson

not by the illusory paint of light

but by the blood of humans

the slaughtered women and children…

Over the vistas of a sinking world

would be the black clouds,

burgeoning from the pain of the souls,

Man suspected all along it was hell

this place he called the earth,

But entrapped in the magnetism

of his richly phantasmagoria

he had come to believe

through the art of self-deception

that this was indeed his heaven!

The flowers will bloom no longer

but enchanting weeds will thrive,

the poisonous fruits of hatred,

that bear the smoky smell of human flesh

with frosty tears in lieu of dewdrops…

My dear child!

this isn't the glorious earth

that enticed you in your foetal dreams

as you levitated above the amniotic waters,

The planet of the miracle called life

the specially endowed blue dot

that the aliens hope to visit someday!

This is a giant grave

though not spacious enough to hold

the demons of a mutated mankind,

The water bodies here are barren

with paints enlivening the deadness,

This is the incinerator of memories

where entire civilisations are erased,

a battleground from prehistory

where boundary lines are drawn in blood,

This is where violent myths are defeated

by the heartless gore of reality,

The gods sleep as the men dance

insanely to the rhythm of death!

The dead philosophers had searched in vain

for the allegory in violence…

My child, my child!

This is not the paradise you hoped for

they don't need you here,

unless you don the devil's mask

to be an impassive automaton!

Do not leave the cradle

it will help you will live in the bunker

in perpetual fear and anxiety,

Do not leave the womb, if possible,

as the lullabies won't ring true anymore

once you are wrapped in falsehood…

Keep your bright eyes tightly shut,

to embrace the reality of darkness,

lest you fall like a fly into the entrapment

of the alluring illusion of light…

I...

I'm nothing but

an atom of the seasons,

I'm in the warm body of summer

as the rustling grass blade

the nest of a wriggly worm!

I'm in the coldness of winter

as the footprint of a vagabond

on the slithering sleet...

I'm in the flora of the spring

as the enticing smile on a leaf

reminiscing the solstice...

I'm that rain drop in autumn

the blood of parturition in the skies,

trapped in the tabernacle of emotions...

I'm in the darkness

that abounds in earth-less space

the extraterrestrial aether,

an element of space-less light...

A NAMELESS COLOUR

What's the colour of death?

Some say it's black

the drapery of darkness

that walls the realm of the dead…

To some others it's white

austere and pure

the luminescent apparition

that infiltrates the night…

Whatever it may be

the innate sense of death

is the bitterness of winter,

the silent coldness amidst the wails

the wanton tears of frost

untouched by scorching summer,

Where the air is suffocating

gripped by the melancholy,

where the fallen flowers in the room

smell of the subtle perfumes of death,

where the shards from broken hearts

are scattered over the bleeding floor,

where weary eyes search for the soul

in the catacombs of severe insomnia,

where ant men trundle along greasy walls

seeking the evasive solace in grief,

There life becomes a dreamer's fantasy

a charade where fate throws the dice

to vain men who are entranced in the game

The season breaks the window panes

with its unforgiving icy cold fingers,

A nameless season that has dead flowers

it feels like hard winter, though…

A LETTER FROM THE QUICKSANDS

I feel them ebbing away

into the distant shores,

through their sociable smiles

into the islands of reclusiveness…

Like a random wave of rain

the saccharine friendships

crescendo with excitement,

and just when the fever grips

it abruptly pauses, and then

it flatlines inexorably

into another lifeless relationship!

What is held as a passion

within the chambers of the heart

remains deep and personal

untouched by the superfluous…

The illusion ought not be believed

as it is bound to emptiness,

Friendship may be another shield

just to combat the estrangement,

Nothing stays on the wall forever

the wall itself is to disappear

into the abyss of impassable darkness...

Within the shell of self-pity

the wounded man takes shelter

just so that he could survive,

braving the hostile coldness

with the embers of hope in the hearth...

Do the leaves tremble every moment

out of happiness or fear, no one knows;

The passivity that governs the living

is shared by the dying leaf and the man...

The wave leaves the shore

never to return to the same form again,

the reincarnations that are fascinating belong only to the realm of dreams

too surreal and forgotten rapidly at dawn...

The seas remain unperturbed,

passive to the fragile sentiments...

The seagulls prayerfully circle the skies

rekindling their hopes of life,

Meanwhile the frivolous rain dissipates

into some broken rays of sunshine,

convoluting the solid faces of reality

into thin abstracts of imperfections…

Futile are the prevarications

to attenuate the twists of destiny,

The shore that the leaf has flown to

awaits the man, naked and newly born…

A few remain on the shore

like the shells of long dead molluscs

The conch has a music within,

a heart that beats to its own rhythm…

Over the shards of the memories

of the spent joys of the yesterdays,

the bare footed man moves heavily,

slowed down by the searing melancholy…

The language of love is silent

a music without the written notes,

Waves arrive and they recede

depositing the seaweeds of yesteryears,

And one could only hope in despair

that the winds that bring forth the waves

would permeate the anguished soul

to birth something new and nascent,

an unbreakable natural natal bond

that with a divine grace would redefine

the age-old cast iron rules of longevity…

A POUND OF THOUGHT?

Thought cannot be quantified

with a weight or a measure,

There is no volume in it

nor is it hollow!

Then what's it exactly

thought, that shapes the man

whipper snipping the weedy path

leading to his so-called destiny?

It has no exactness

an anatomical definition,

It isn't physically solid

but is stronger than any material,

It is not a drop in the ocean

but the ocean itself in a drop…

What happens to the thoughts

of a dead and decaying man?

His cache of memories,

the processed experiences

within the matter of his brain?

Within the nebulae

are there those unspoken thoughts

yet to be born, but will never be!

Lost in a phase of infinite translation,

the black box never to be recovered

from the ashes of bygone lives?

A picture is a thought

it is not quantifiable,

Whether it imparts a profound experience

or a scratch on the surface, is immaterial

What matters is the thought

genuine but amorphous,

that creates an illusion of a visual

that tugs at the heart

of a discerning viewer…

Thought defies the rules of mathematics

and the scales of semantics,

It is there in the silence, the pauses

between words,

All that could be said

is that there is more thought

in the unspoken spaces,

the glances, the sighs,

the silent darkness of the corridors

than that is expressed through words…

A DATE WITH A POT OF TEA

Why do you commute everyday

to the corner where the nice man

pours hot tea from the samovar?

Why do you relish the concoction,

of boiled milk and dark leaves

that has no spoonfuls of sugar

but is still delicately saccharine?

Why do your tired eyes wander

like a child in his nursery playpen

searching for novel excitement?

Why do you loiter around the tree

throwing half glances at the skies

where a rain is about to take birth?

Why do you listen to the voices

of those random strangers in love

as they warm up their pining hearts?

Why do you feel so detached

though for a tiny slice of time

much smaller than the fried snack?

Why do you sense your heart venting

fumes of its unspoken thoughts

like the vapours from the tea pot?

Why do you gravitate to the place

as if no others serve real tea

deepening the roots like the aged tree?

Why do you long for the morning

to be there and to help yourself

to that freshly brewed elixir?

Why do you hope for the day to end

to be there to renew the memory

with another sip, as the dusk fades away?

You are seeking a memory

of care, love and affection,

You are rooting like a newborn

to the warmth of your mother,

You are a man in solitude

but your instinct is to be social,

to be with others, to fill your senses

with their chats and laughter!

You are acutely aware of the brevity of life

truncated like the autumn leaf,

You need to be alive every moment

marking the milestones of dawn and dusk,

The man is a provider of good food

that touches your inner taste buds

as well as your engraved memory…

You are wont to be there on time

a habit conferring a survival advantage,

It is not just the joy of piping hot tea

but the creation of a tantalising memory

that gets you there, to be alive

to be there, to finish the cup of tea

To pour it again, before you are gone!

A CONFESSION

Who should I confess to

the misdeeds, the misfortunes

out of my own making?

Where's the confessional

is it up there, atop the mountains

which speak directly to the heavens?

Is it below the ocean, on its floor

studded with pearls unseen?

If there be no heaven or hell

should I really confess at all?

What difference would it make

to the unfortunate outcomes

of events that have happened already?

The river cannot seek the stream

the stream cannot covet the raindrop,

What has been born has to exist

so too the events that shape lives,

they are there, solid and pertinent,

So should one be penitent

if all is a design, all is random

and man is just a cog in the wheel

that rolls over murky lands to eternity?

But the feeling of guilt is hurtful

it wounds the heart, it bleeds,

it upsets the equilibrium

that thus far had kept him going,

as if it's staging a vocal protest

viciously stabbing at the core

of the uncertainty, at the aftermath

of a vicariously negligent event…

The mind yearns for a closure

as is the case with every trauma,

But like the new life

birthed through unending labour,

the trauma never gets to the exit door

instead bifurcating into an unclear path

that's riddled with more intense guilt

and futile self-loathing…

The confession is not an admission of guilt

but it's a coping stratagem

a candid conversation with the soul,

to open up newer avenues

to shrink the remoteness,

to convert the otherness

into an intimacy, not for extenuating

but for the realisation that a bond exists

between the sin and the sinner

however remote that may be in reality…

The confession is the token of realisation

of that relation, which could alchemise

the potion, the panacea

for the self-inflicted mental wounds…

IF ONLY...

If only man could converse

with the silence of his own shadow,

If only he could pause

to savour the silvery droplets of light

toddling along the floor,

If only he could see

the many subtle shades

of life within the greens,

the joy of yellow in a dying sunflower,

If only he could dream

for a sleep resplendent with dreams,

If only he could look at the wall

to realise the needles would someday stall

to vanish from the dial forever,

If only he could feel the pain

of having to leave the world whilst alive,

If only he could see the child

that belongs to a world of happiness

within the open prisons of misery,

If only he could be cognisant

of the lone child in the mirror

the trueness of his own unspoken self,

If only he could believe in that one myth

of a serendipitously preserved self-image,

If only he could revisit that locked room

where his only toy in rags awaits him,

If only he could feel his tears

augmenting the haziness of the cobwebs,

If only he is choked and agonised

by the dust of his ignored past,

If only he could sit back and relish

the children playing on theatre stage

applauding with unabashed eccentricity,

If only he could dissolve into that shadow

and take flight into the other side of light,

Then only he would visualise

the panorama of what's called life,

free from the spectres of egoism,

the vainglorious clash of ideologies,

and unchain himself with conviction,

to begin his long delayed journey

from being a sacrificial animal to a human…

NO ROOM

"Too constrained!!!

Not enough space

for the two of us!"

so claims the demon,

the vile amorphous ego

the resident within!

The cottage is shrinking

into a microscopic atom,

the walls are no longer walls

but neat rows of bars

unbendable shiny metal,

morphing into a cage!

The greenery is burning

the fumes stink of flesh

as the cries of the orphaned

their thin necks strangled

suffocate the air…

The gorge is expanding

the water has the colour of blood,

the demon is still thirsty

feasting over the misery…

The crimson skies open up

revealing the darkness within,

Man becomes blind

enhancing the devil's visual acuity,

The hell is visible

with its eternal fires,

Over the tender bones of children

are erected its formidable walls,

The atom craves for implosion

to release the demon,

and to attain the alluring hell!

At that moment the gong strikes

and the dream ends,

leaving the ashes on the sill…

The cottage is intact

but its walls are no longer innocent

the carpeted floors too cold

the dark mist outside foreboding…

A STAR ALIVE ON EARTH

Minds of the youthful

brimming with energy

boundless and electrifying!

Ready to fly and soar high

piercing the veneered blueness

of the sun drenched skies!

Looking askance at the norms

ever so eager to defy the rules

and bend the concepts of time!

The society of the youth

is a world in its own right,

unchained from dogmas

and heedless of the future!

Many a man, old and dying

have craved for that chalice

for a drop of the magical potion

of dynamic youthfulness,

Many a leaf turned gold

with the advent of autumn

has hoped for the same,

But all they got in the end

was a cold embrace

from the leafy chest of a moist earth…

The stallions that they once rode upon

have abandoned them to their fate,

men walk the salty shores

with painfully naked warty feet

vain seekers of the holy grail of age

so as not to become frail,

Written on the parchments

of their gloomy wrinkled faces

clouded with searing self-doubts,

are not the ancient alphabets of wisdom

but an insatiable greed for longevity,

to be the breakers of the rules of nature

the wizardly benders of time

a dystopian monstrous parody

of the natural bloom of youth…

THE HALO OF A NIGHT

The skies tilt and close in,

the crimson smile vanishing

at the confluence of the seas;

The dawn has come a full circle

as the birds paying their homage

coo in a prayerful mode…

It has rained hard all day

the heavens mourning over nothingness

The trees stricken with grief

danced in a wild frenzy

like an orphaned child's tantrum

pulling the leafy hairs apart

until felled to the soil at last

by the insufferable exhaustion…

The third act of the drama

was written in the ink of silence,

an interminable pause ensues

drowning the gasps of the dying star;

The soul sinks at the horizon

over the ruins of an ancient shipwreck,

A wave of solemnity spreads

over the chaotic fluttering heart

of the deeply turbulent seas…

The mariners are making progress

rowing the bloody beaked albatross,

The colossal shadow of the martyred

densifies the approaching darkness,

the under-sketches of ultramarine blue

coalesce with the solidifying blackness,

the seas dissolving into a dream

of a fiery rain in the future,

where monsters regurgitate flames of fury…

The great Poseidon has gone to rest

after centuries of exasperating Godship

to sleep in the giant ornate water graves;

oblivious to the spirits of the new world…

Theseus, the warlord, the conqueror

sleeps in the tomb of the vanquished;

A mortally wounded warrior of Troy

yearns for the pristine shores of yore

bled by the stiletto of nostalgia…

Through the slit in the artery of history

the memories exit to find their way

into the dream of the marooned sailor;

The isle is bucolic but is eerily calm

submerged for eons in forgetfulness,

The night awaits the lonely lark

to breathe out a mellifluous tune

into the expansive clouds of darkness…

BETWEEN A MYTH AND A STORY

The rules of death:

It has no god

not even a demigod,

It is nothing holy

or even vaguely spiritual,

It has no back page

no aftermath, no "ever-afters"

Only an one-sided print

in black and bold letters

"Death"

expected or not,

tragic to the spectators

moved to tears by the distress,

or comic to the unaffected,

Yet it is a miracle by all means

the stoppage of heartbeats

No more wasteful breaths

after the terminal agony,

the fruitless desperation to hold on…

The tantalising is over

the illusive grapes of afterlife

no longer have the allure;

Only abstruse unholy darkness

a lavish stroke of pitch darkness,

right across the board,

putting the cells to sleep…

A dreamless one,

darker than any earthly night

the stars wiped off the invisible skies!

The labour pains of life

to birth fruits, one after the other

to achieve, to win, be relentless

to undo emotions of the heart

casting it with wrought iron,

all those tactics of the living

meeting a cold end,

The gargantuan ship in dreams

carrying the famed gold

of the ancient extinct lands

sinking with spontaneity

into an abyss of nothingness…

Does not the fluttering heart

on the precipice of a flatline,

realise the depth of "a moment,"

the unearthly nature of music,

the knowing that the sculpted one

that he was, is crumbling into dust,

becoming the fragment of a fossil

in the fathomless pit

the hole in the universe

that he has always been?

Does the trueness of vision

arrive after the curtains are drawn

in the deepest core of blindness?

Does he realise with a searing pain

that he was never a mystery,

but that it was his own choice

to conceal it as a myth?

That he didn't write his own

but stole somebody else's story

borrowing the attires of another

that truly didn't fit him at heart,

A choice without regrets thus far

that is impaled in stakes of guilt…

Does he feel that coldness

the aloneness of incarceration?

the smiles were endearing

the joys felt all too real

yet nothing was enduring

Does he catch a vain glimpse

of even a word that's written

that's his own,

but left buried and ignored

in the inert waters of nonchalance

till it is too late to realise?

PHANTOM OF A GRAFFITI

It is indeed good to travel

as a close knit group, a union

bound by that common thread

of unassuming gentle camaraderie!

The grumpy engine rumbles along

the long winding track, worn out

by centuries of peddling of ideas,

The evolving power of reasoning

mitigates the risk of derailing

of the vagrant human minds,

shining the incisive torchlight

into the darkness of the future…

Like the newborn rigorously latching

to the exhausted mother's breasts

thirsty for the taste of colostrum,

man perseveres on the track

anxiously febrile to get to the roots

of the primitive plant that's his existence…

He grows downwards, into the depths

past the manured nourishing layers

digging past the tender formative years,

to the entombed times of old

where the shadow of the bud, a blastocyst

is encased within a fragile eggshell…

From those darkest depths of blindness

he can hear, though faint like a murmur

the mighty engine threading its way

through the indispensable trials,

the innumerable merciless cacti of life…

In that spiritual well tiled with darkness

ornate with the etchings of dead seashells

he feels the beauty of companionship

with his soul, an unparalleled vision

of the mind bonding with the universe…

The magnificence of life's illusions

dwarfed and dwindled into nothingness

with the mounts of the paradises dismantled

to bite the dust in the valleys of darkness,

The silhouette of the timeless man

armoured with the shadows of the night

wounded, scarred and stubborn

is graffitied into the endless tunnels

littered along the creaky rail tracks…

The man with the indefatigable spirit of enquiry

emerging from the labyrinthine roots,

adapting through the art of unlearning,

to scramble up the shreds of originality

that he had long lost in the consuming woods…

He is a sight to behold, thinks the driver

a singular figure cloaked in the darkness

unclaimed by the ravaging raids of time,

"an immovable sculpture" in the museum of life…

The driver shouldn't sleep, but think he must

as the vigorous engine ignores the buttons

and creatively finds its own track,

like the children riding horses in a carousel!

The man in the tunnel is a belief

a phantom, a vestige of ancient thoughts,

born from the curiosity of a child's vision,

covered in the moist mud of the earth,

with roots snaking out of the heart…

uncouth but original, raw and difficult

he must be, the mind being unchained

from the lighthouses of civilisation!

Thus thinks the driver amid the tumults

of an engine that's carving its way,

through the tunnel saturated with the night;

It is that time, when the graffitis come alive

the immobile find their rudimentary legs

to infuse a breath of life into the torpid hours,

lest the driver falls into that deep sleep

the engine becoming a passing dream

from which he may wake up suddenly

with roots emanating from the still heart…

LINES! LINES!

Lines! lines

that never end

nervy serpentines!

with flocks of people

huffing and puffing

curious about nothing!

The barricade is invisible

the stocky built guard smirks,

restless machines beep,

customers come and go,

securing their things,

merging into another line…

The traffic of footfalls

from morning to night

that keeps the earth awake…

Clusters of families

with children of all ages

and their sleepy eyed dolls,

hardly awake in their pajamas!

The formations of lines

dissolving into a constellation,

Like streams hugging the river

are the ongoing movements,

Lines! convoluted tracks

winding around the tedium

rigidly disciplined

like platoons of soldiers

marching in their trainers!

Lines parallel to each other

with no bridge of a smile,

with an over-refined politeness,

discomfited with strangeness

receding to their opaque shells

while pretending to be socialising!

Nothing really stands out

in the bizarrely linear crowd,

except the children

caught up in the long line

with their sleepy eyed dolls!

AN ESSENTIAL JOURNEY

If time and tide allows you

to travel back in time,

Do not forget to get to that shade

of the lushly haired old Palmyra tree,

that still stands with its head tall

weathering the heat and storms!

Do not hesitate to pinch the crystals

of the early spring shine

that bedeck the meadow over there!

Do not restrain yourself with vanity

feel free to climb the lemon yellow walls

without fear of abrading your sallow skin

whilst sneaking into the yard like a thief!

Do not knock on those varnished doors

as they has always been left open,

for you to waddle into the room!

Do not let the hurtful knees prevent you

from taking a seat in that low bench,

let the cartilage utter the cursing rattles

as you strive to squeeze into the space!

Do stoop forward to keep your ears pressed

hard against the top of the desk,

as you may hear the roars from the throats

of those in the bloom of childhood!

Do have a sudden flash of an afterthought

that you've forgotten the cache of books,

perspire, fret over what is about to happen!

Do not be afraid of the passing shadows

as you're immersed in the magic of reverie

A memory that is never tired of life

that's what you're!

Memories are unseen, you're shielded

Do not rest till you are done with your adventure!

Go back for more,

to savour more of that joy and pain,

Weep over the lost days like a child

It will only do you good,

The pain doesn't maul or scar you

for, it is the rehabilitation of your inner self,

So, bon voyage, back to where your soul belongs…

THE SHINE

The sleepy meadow is awash

with the gold of sunshine

giving the impression of summer!

But the cold fingers of winter

prod the chest of the traveller

reminding him of the reality…

The juxtaposed images of nature

reflects the contrasts in life,

the varying shades of emotions

on display from dawn to dusk!

Unforeseen to the naked mortal eyes

that are taken in by arty visuals

is the coldness within the candescence,

the bitterness in the shell of enticement…

But for the journey to go on

one ought to believe at least in himself,

though affected by the lure of colours

that abound in the surrounding world;

His soul is a monochrome image

that's not drawn into the mirage,

but he surrenders to the deception

as he is none but another mortal!

Has any animal ever sensed

the specks of gold within the mighty rock?

Only man has, as he is captivated

by the irradiance of his dreams,

He believes in the ambitions within him

to follow his hunch to hunt the gold,

though well aware of the brevity of his life;

Through the smokescreen of contrasts

he navigates, attracted and obsessed,

to the lure that he believes is his destiny!

Past the burial ground of memories

and the illusive landscapes sculpted in time

he soldiers along with a passionate heart

in the hopes of striking pure gold!

There is fire in his eyes, reflecting the metal,

the glow that hides the stillness within it…

THE CUBE

Would it crumble,

this cube placed in my hands

into the dust that it is

in the light of reality?

What do I see inside,

a hidden rabbit warren?

My eyes are unsurprisingly weary

the vision doesn't stretch too far…

The boy is gleefully playing

his body appears to be upside down

or is it my deceptive vision tilting?

his cheeks are rosy with sweat…

It must be the peak of summer

I feel the excitement of holidays!

He's dangling on the swing

and climbing atop the neem tree…

Do I not see the tenting sky
replete with the sun and the stars
within his own tiny kingdom,
inconspicuous to the outer world!

He is chasing the moonlight
that encircles his energetic feet!
I note that the leaves are evergreen
even when night drops into his world…

Like a colt who has sensed danger
he springs to his feet and vanishes
suddenly rising a mount of dust
when his eyes meet mine!

My words are frozen in my throat
I want to cry aloud but I can't!
I want to be near him, at least for a moment
to feel his curly hair and liquid black eyes…

He must have burrowed in deep

to where no human gaze can reach,

The child naturally has magic

that morphs him into a stag in a flash!

I feel like a wasted shred of paper

sore at heart and tearful in my eyes,

I don't know why, but I feel all alone

like all the winters have struck me at once!

I drop the cube to the ground in despair

believing it would break into pieces,

The sense of loss overwhelming me

I lost faith in the promise of life…

But it was not obliged to gravity,

it had risen above me like a ghostly figure,

then swirling into a spiral of dust,

"I'm real, I'm real!" I cried in vain…

SAILING OVER THE LOST WORLD

From the ornate chalice

I've drunk the elixir of nonchalance!

To be not myself, to be calm,

detached like a kite in ashy skies

as I glide over the ruins

the dilapidated nests of the past,

where memories still flickering with life

lie shattered into pieces,

to be trampled over by the young…

The garden created by foresight

with millions of exuberant flowers

cleverly overlay the ravaged land!

But the deception is transparent

I see through the visual spectacle

like the strokes of reality within a dream,

The sadness of having lost my childhood

the flimsiness of the glassy cable car

that interconnects the forgotten eras,

and the unforgiving air of melancholy…

The thorns are sharp and precise

lancing the core of the heart

like darts aimed by deft hands!

The ruins rise their heads from the ashes

the wreckage is bathed in red,

from the blood draining from the hearts

which were once young and boyish,

Time has been violent in its tactics

to demolish the sculpted memories

to bury in mass graves of forgetfulness…

The past is crimson from the war

It is the blood of warriors who've lost the battle,

forced to surrender their grounds to the diktats of time…

THE BOY WHO DIDN'T SELL DREAMS

The dream merchant

met the boy on the way

He was a poor orphan

sickly with rickety chest,

The man feeling sorry for him

and moved by his appearance,

took out the bottle of dreams

from the goat skin bag;

The boy gazed in wonder

with a tide of joyful curiosity

in his liquid black eyes,

The merchant distilled the potion

and counted from one to three

as the drops entered the boy's eyes,

The kaleidoscope was ready

as the boy shook with excitement;

He peeped inside the cylinder

to delight at the optical spectacle!

No one knew what was inside the dream

not even the merchant of dreams,

as it was left to the beholder's eyes

to savour the choicest of visuals!

But the merchant believed for sure

that the vision excited the men and women

bringing them heights of joy!

But the boy didn't seem impressed

as his face showed no amusement

when he quietly returned the instrument;

The merchant was piquant

and gently ventured to ask him

why he was not rapturous

by the sight of a beautiful dream!

To which the boy calmly replied

looking at the hills in the distance

to which the birds were taking flight:

"My life is more beautiful than a dream!"

He didn't need the wisdom

from the ancient book of alchemy

to create a world of dreams

just to see something beautiful

and to feel happy in life!

The child naturally was wise and free

who saw beauty in everything in his life,

The world belonged to him

like a piece of candy in his palm…

WRITTEN ON THE SEAS

Only the mind sees

the entirety of a dream;

What one gets glimpses of

are fragments of the story,

some of the many streams

that feed into that optical sea!

What is created poetically

from the tabernacle of memories

is buried deep within the mind;

How often do dreams recur

with the same intense rigour?

Not often does that happen

it ought to something sublime

or fearful and pathological;

The bygones are juxtaposed

with the newer impressions

extracted from the wells of life

to create yet another experience,

a silent symphony of the senses…

One bumps into many a face

while within that misty world,

characters that've changed

their names and attires different;

It could be the multiple reflections

of the same persona

in the shards of the broken mirror,

The person being oneself

superimposed on other faces,

Their vexations are his own

their answerless questions

the intrigue on their faces

Everything come from within him

untrammelled as the dreamer sleeps!

The mind sees it all

pondering over the dilemmas

dissecting the ethics and morals

of that convoluted visual saga;

Does not one see the pensiveness

in the mood of the early morning

as the dust clears from the eyes?

Another chapter of the day begins

imbibing the threads of the past,

like the elixir of dreams

synthesised from the elements within…

A BABY DOLL

A baby doll

that's not just a doll

But almost a baby

the skin so soft and supple

the cheeks an alluring purple,

the cute face grimacing

and is bursting to cry aloud,

like an autumn thunder

to stir up and awaken the world

that's lost in a deep slumber!

The phantasm of a human life

as if birthed from a womb

is sadly a passing dream,

of the exhausted mother

drenched in her own tears

She, who has lost her child,

that was not a wooden doll

but a real life,

a beautiful but short-lived butterfly…

IT GETS DARK EARLY

These days it gets dark early

The light flashes for moments

through the leafy windows

and vanishes in an undue haste!

The light is no longer tinted gold

but only imparts a feeling,

A sensation of thrifty warmth

shrouded by the cold winds;

Through the heavily blindfolded skies

overcast and about to burst,

the light transmits messengers

draped in a misty whiteness,

The impression is that of a moon

a gigantic spherical piece of sky

sitting silently by the window…

as the wintry day ebbs away

aware of the brevity of its life;

The coldness is not just in the air

but in the face of the white light

peaceful and disquieting at once…

How conscious a man is

about the frivolity of the moment,

the predicament of his existence!

How subtly his senses are attuned

to the fragile shades of light

the changing colours of seasons

as if they exist within him!

The light plays with passing shadows

like children frolicking in the park,

If only man could fly with the birds

and not within a technological bubble,

he could follow the trajectory of the light,

careful not to burn his fluttering wings!

They say the soul has no wings

(only the angels do!)

yet the soul of man flies, he believes so,

the wings must be within the man himself

folded and stored like a spotty umbrella

only to be used when it rains after death…

Man converses with his own thoughts

entranced by the image in the mirror,

engaging in a pretend play

like a child stranded indoors on a rainy day

who is in good company with his own playfulness,

he plays to be less mindful of the darkness,

as the sunlight swims across the river

fading into a deep crimson shadow…

THE RAIN AFTER THE FALL

The sky is mysteriously dark

like the wing of a giant raven,

The winds emerge from nowhere

venting their pent-up anxieties,

as fluttering waves of rains

crosshatch the papery terrain;

The sounds of the human world

is replaced by the music of the rains,

It waxes and wanes rhythmically

like the fluctuating mood of winter,

The guileless child plays indoors

pretending to treat the sick doll in a frock!

After a crescendo of downpour

geared up by the lustful gusts

there enters the interlude of silence,

The murmurs have paused for the moment,

the birds venture to peek outside

with their extraordinary prescience;

Flowers drop over the fallen angels

lying buried in the memories of autumn,

Rain brings back the bygone years

when it used to rain hard, all day long!

There used to be mud in the streets

in the gutters where frogs gambolled,

as the humble millipede sat on the mossy wall!

The colourful umbrellas were always porous

and children drenched themselves with abandon!

The rains came to get rid of the tedium

ushering in the waves of vim and vigour,

Nothing could beat the music of the rain

bearing down on the resilient roof,

the one soundtrack that would put any child to sleep!

It is the memory of those beautiful nights

where one sumptuously slept

cozying up beside the tightly shut window

that the rains bring as gift every year

and this time it is no different!

A PREHISTORIC DREAM

I find my space

on the cold parapet

and gaze at the ancient sky,

the submerged sea of stars

foretelling the pre-winter rain…

Lives breathe and speak

in their distinct languages

from the creek and the bush,

the wet unwitting grass blades

bonding with opportunistic weeds,

as the febrile winds of autumn

smoothly melt into a pallid coldness;

The silence of the nocturnal crickets

who usually sing in chorus

is a bit disconcerting!

The larks have flown to rest

somewhere deep in the thickets,

The rebellious one dares to croon

piercing the veil of the night;

I sit back and think

about the days before history,

when the naked man and woman

cozied up by the kindled fire,

What could they've been thinking about?

the pervasive darkness and its shadowy beasts

or the peaceful interlude of the night

that brings relief for a sweltering hot day?

Did they really believe they would wake up

to see the sun rising over the Savannah?

Every rustling leaf, every chattering wind

would have instilled anxiety in them,

about what lies behind those sounds

the death that lurks in the shadows,

Yet, they managed to ease their heads to sleep

and perhaps, they dreamt too,

futuristic giants from the catacombs of time

may have appeared in those visuals,

with green eyes and blue tongues,

bewitching but intimidating!

They may have fought off death with all their might

whilst still entrapped in their dream world,

only to wake up at dawn and realise

the harsh and bitter truth of their own mortality!

Beside them, in the embers of a dying fire

there slept the shreds of a bygone dream…

THE STATE OF BEING HAPPY?

What is happiness?

Apart from the literal etymology

precisely what does it mean?

They say they're "happy"

Maybe feeling "good"

and genuinely "contended,"

Maybe they've been plain lucky

striking gold at every turn!

Maybe they feel "light at heart"

with no heaviness of a rocky life,

Is that so?

"His happiness is not mine"

is how the adage goes!

What does that mean?

Every sense of happiness is unique,

It isn't a feeling of satiety

or sleeping on a bag of riches,

Being acclaimed and stupendously successful

probably has nothing to do with it;

Happiness cannot be herded

bound together by a single thread,

It does not always bring forth a smile

for the face has little to do with the heart;

Laughter is only a visible symbol

it could mean many things!

Is the child a sign of happiness

carefree and unaffected

blooming with innocence?

He too has anxieties

but they're regarded as trifles,

less relevant in the world of adults;

Maybe, he could tell us

what his concept of happiness is,

describe his perception in his own words!

It could be the sight of magic

or a sugary candy floss

A victory in the cricket field,

something rewarding for the young brain,

Or maybe we've got it wrong all along?

The child maybe happy not out of his choice

it is simply a state in being in childhood!

Could a common man ever be happy,

or a prisoner languishing in a jail

or a homeless destitute in the street?

That the world is full of worries

doesn't mean everyone is worrying everyday

They have their moments

of sadness, which dissipate with time,

Many could be pathologically anxious

requiring a doctor's remedy,

But many could just be getting along

with the lives they've got,

Is that a state of happiness too,

a sense of general well-being?

An artist could be in a creative frenzy

spending his energy onto the canvas,

Is he happy during or after his venture?

So, the definitions are many,

billions of them for that many people!

Everyone is happy or sad in his or her own way,

depending very much on the individual circumstances;

One could talk about "absolute" happiness

that they believe the hermit has in his retreat,

in the radiant eyes within the steeliness of his face…

Does renouncement give rise to happiness,

A state of sublime detachment

which could be (perhaps be) synonymous with happiness?

We don't know for certain

But one thing we do know

is that nature is always in meditation

even when storms build inside the skies

or the interiors of the earth begin to shake;

The silence of the trees could be happiness

so is the breeze rustling the leaves

and the river that flows in the woods,

Human happiness may not be distinct from other lives

though he happens to equate his wellness

to the quantum of wealth and other materials;

The art of being alive is happiness

the joy of the world is happiness,

It is not the satiety of the plentiful

but the peace and harmony at heart…

It is ultimately a reward for the mind

that is borne out of nothing in particular,

It is a unique state of being within nothingness,

It is not a quantifiable element

in a clever mathematical equation!

It could be the state of being in a dream

barricaded from the mundanity of life!

The more "it" is chased around like a stag in the woods

the more evasive it becomes!

If left alone, it would arrive naturally

one day, at the door of the mind,

Not as a meaty commodity to be pampered

but as a perception, abstract and sublime…

THE ARTFUL WAR

War

kills women and children

even babies unborn in wombs,

Lives are erased like flies

and the bond of humanity decimated…

War

displaces the hapless people

their lands made uninhabitable

with mushroom clouds of souls

rising high above like mountains…

War

is man's primitive weapon

It has no conscience

It needs no reason

The poison of visceral hatred is enough

for man to inflict pain on another…

Wars

gave the painters of yore their subjects

the flamboyance of hellish violence

with thousands of boots on horses' hoofs

their war cries piercing the gallery's walls!

Wars

made the poet a philosopher

compelling him to pen words,

Verses with the light of insightful wisdom;

But as with everything good in mankind

they're to be quietly forgotten,

as man cannot abandon his love for war!

THE STORY OF THE CLOUDS

I used to wonder

what held the clouds up so high

firmly in their starry heights,

The giant transforming figures

beyond the reach of my fingers!

I used to believe

that they were paintings

glued on to the blue ceilings,

The sky being the wall

of some master painter's gallery!

I used to follow them

with innocent curiosity in my eyes,

fascinated by the nebulous fluffs

morphing into cottony shapes and figures

forming a constellation in the skies!

I knew their faces turned dark

when the rains gathered within them,

They had befriended the furious storms

the fearful thunder and lightning,

I could only hope their anger would resolve!

I learnt that life wouldn't happen

without the fortune of the rainfall,

The clouds were mother nature's breasts

Feeding earth's children, the parched fields

the milk of life… water!

I learnt later, to my despair

that the skies were my imagination,

They didn't exist, nor did their alluring colours,

The illusion of light seemed like real

if there's anything such as reality!

I still watch with the child's lens in my eyes

the mysterious clouds passing by,

the chains of rivers they form,

wondering what messages they could be carrying

Knowing well that it is my mind telling a story!

ON A PLATFORM ONE WINTRY NIGHT

We live in a world

that's over medicated

intoxicated with optical wonders

We tell this to ourselves!

We are languid, yet

find it hard to sleep

even inside the finest of quilt;

We stand on these platforms

that would transfer us

to our places of preference,

The platform is solid

but it feels like soft jelly,

slowly invading the legs

The train is a marvel

It is a delight to watch it coming

through the icy cold tracks

as the snow is wafted out swiftly;

The medication is kicking in

(it is supposed to!)

to invite the reluctant sleep

to share the bed,

Otherwise the train might be missed!

It's wintry stillness outside

We hold our hands together

as our heads dig into the pillows

squeezing gently the duck feathers,

We're over medicated

illusive is the optics

We are phantasms that are expendable,

Like the flakes of snow

shovelled away by the train of time,

We tell ourselves

It is time to sleep, or more accurately

it is high time we slept,

(We correct ourselves)

The soporific effects of the night

fail to cast the spell

on either of our minds,

We run parallel to the tracks

though our legs feel like jellies

trying to garner some strength

which we seem to have lost!

We puff and pant

knowing well we won't make it,

Our heads spin as they sink

deeper into the hollows of the pillows,

Our eyes flicker like torches

that are running out of batteries,

the oscillating light that emanates

betraying the glimmers of our hope:

A hope that we both share, together

myself and sleep,

that we may not miss the train, after all…

WHAT THE MIRROR SAID

The music flows

from the nocturnal lyre

The man runs in a frenzy

not from fear, but excitement

that he's unable to contain,

His legs spring like a stag

from one tent to another

The red dens of miniatures,

memories sculpted in time,

bathed in golden yellow light…

He has seen them before

but the experience is new,

more delightful and delicate

punctuated by the music

that's mystifying and enticing;

Who has created these

the sculptor within the mind?

or an eccentric who hides himself

in the wilderness, he wonders!

He can see it from above

the dreamy city of dreams

with its innumerable dwellings

lit up and shining bright

to be seen from the heavens

that are eons away…

The harbour of his memories

the treasures of his past!

He runs wild

to that tent that awaits him,

the only one with mirrors,

dimly lit unlike the others…

Who does he meet in there

behind those crimson curtains

Resembling the sunset clouds?

The image is of a human being,

of his own self,

in the truthful honesty of the mirror,

he sees the metamorphosis

with dreams in his eyes

that he's no longer an adult,

but a child…

DR. BOBAN RAMESAN

23/09/2025

ABOUT THE AUTHOR

Dr Boban Ramesan is a family physician based in Brisbane who has a penchant for art and literature. He was born in 1977 in Kerala ,India and completed his postgraduate training in the United Kingdom where he worked as a family physician before relocating to Brisbane in 2015 with his family. He has published two volumes of poetry and collections of philosophical essays in India and has conducted multiple art exhibitions which have been critically acclaimed. His poetry has influences from the narrative styles of Edgar Allan Poe and William Blake and he is also an ardent admirer of the works of the English romantics. To him his literary journey is essentially a philosophical quest, he finds his poetic endeavours self-explorative with the surrealistic dreamy subtleties instilled into his art works thereby creating a fascinating cycle of synergism. He believes in the poetic side of Impressionism infusing the imageries of spectacular vibrancy of nature in the eternal mystery of the human condition unravelling novel fascinating facets of the beauty of life, a collaborative union of poetry and art that effectively brings forth another sub-genre of literature.

As the adage goes

"If life doesn't have a meaning

art most probably has one !...".

www.ingramcontent.com/pod-product-compliance
Lightning Source LLC
Chambersburg PA
CBHW052013070526
44584CB00016B/1735